REPPED

30 DAYS TO A BETTER ONLINE REPUTATION

ANDY BEAL

D1462434

Andy Beal/Marketing Pilgrim LLC
8711 Six Forks Rd, #104-200
Raleigh, NC 27614
www.andybeal.com

Ordering Information:
Quantity sales. Special discounts are available on quantity purchases by corporations, associations, and others. For details, contact the "Special Sales Department" at the address above.

Repped / Andy Beal. —1st ed.
ISBN 13: 978-1493698066
ISBN-10: 1493698060

For my beautiful wife Sheila. It would take an entire book to fully express just how much I love you.

CONTENTS

ACKNOWLEDGEMENTS

IT HAS BEEN six years since I wrote my first book, *Radically Transparent*, and I thought—I may have actually vowed—that I would never write another book. I simply didn't have it in me. Then, during a thirty-minute drive downtown, the concept, structure, content, and title of a new book came to me. I was on my way to the Raleigh Rescue Mission, a Christian emergency and recovery shelter for the homeless where I sit on the Board of Directors as well as teach ukulele classes. You often hear the phrase "divine intervention," but I truly believe this was a case of divine *inspiration*. With that in mind, I would like to first thank God for not only giving me the idea, but giving me the stamina and eloquence to write *Repped*.

Very closely behind, I thank my wonderful wife, Sheila. If God is my rock and foundation, Sheila is the cement that keeps it all together. She's my best friend, my encourager, my career counselor, my spiritual advisor, and my biggest fan. She is the love of my life.

Okay, mushiness aside, let's get to the folks that helped make this book a reality. A big thank you to Erin Jones for daring to be the first person to proofread the raw draft. A thank you to Lisa Lickel for her final copy edits. Thanks also to Scott Wittig and Richie Norton for helping me navigate the publishing world as an author in 2014. I would also like to thank my previous acquisitions editor Willem Knibbe and my previous coauthor Dr. Judy Strauss—without their original support I probably wouldn't now be in the position to publish *Repped*. Thanks also to Brian Solis for writing an excellent foreword to the book.

I would like to take time to thank all of my friends for their support, not just while writing this book, but also during the ups and downs of my career. I know I will forget someone, but that doesn't mean I shouldn't try! Thanks to Frank and Hope Reed, Mat and Holly Siltala, Ted and Eleanor Franks, Mike Grehan, Ben Wills, Lisa Holton, Michael Streko, Michael Gray, David Wallace, Tony Wright, Chris Brogan, Carrie Hill, Jill Whalen, Dana Lookadoo, Arnie Kuenn, David Horner, Lee Odden, Scott Stratten, Janet Driscoll Miller, Joe Hall, Joanna Lord, Brian Clark, Dean Shaw, Matt McGee, Brett Tabke, Ed Shahzade, Rhea Drysdale, Dave Snyder, Simon Heseltine, Eric Enge, Martin Brossman, and Kim Krause Berg.

Wrapping up, a big thank you to all of my family: my mum Val and my nan Maud; my siblings Mat and Sam, Hannah and Kev, Royston and Ayshae; and all my wonderful nieces and nephews. Not forgetting my in-laws: Dickie and Judy; Michelle and David; and Kelton. And, in loving memory of my father, Trevor, and grandfather, Harry.

Lastly, if you've made it this far, I'd like to thank you, dear reader. Not only did you purchase this book, but you also read it, and you read all of acknowledgements above.

Thank you!

FOREWORD

WITH THE SOCIAL web and proliferation of apps, smart phones and always on Internet access, we are becoming a society of accidental narcissists. I don't believe we set out to become self-obsessed and, to be honest, it's not all that bad. Today's digital lifestyle made self-expression not only possible but also acceptable. Selfies! What once would have been frowned upon as anti-social and narcissistic is now a form of everyday self-expression. It's the new emoticon in many ways.

Sharing our lives is easy and it's rewarding as friends, family, and followers react with Likes, shares, comments, et al. With each update we receive positive reinforcement and are heartened to share more. We now are at the center of our own universe and with each day that passes, we share more of our lives and encouragement pushes our behavior toward extroversion. The words privacy and publicity now take on entirely new meanings as we place on display the very thing our ancestors cherished as privileged. With each update, post, selfie, we share a bit of ourselves that in their own way contribute to a semblance of our digital persona. This, though, works for and against us...

Online, just like in the real world, actions and words speak loudly. Unlike real life, though, your digital footprints are there for anyone to find on Google, social networks, and in communities. These disparate pieces are then assembled by employers, schools, friends, lovers, enemies, and anyone and everyone who wish to learn something more about you. Whether pure, sinister, or simply inquisitive, whatever the reason, today these pieces construct a semblance of you and whoever sifts through your online legacy is left to their own surmise. This is too important to leave to chance. Online is the new real world. This is your life.

Getting repped is something we should think about but rarely do. We should be more methodical about what we share and why. But online engagement is teaching us to think in the moment instead of anticipating how those moments collect and assemble into something we didn't initially foresee. Andy Beal is on to something here. And, if we each think deeply about it, we are indeed the masters of our own digital fate by choosing what we share and how we reward those who guide us online. At the same time, we are also the beast of our own burden by sharing whimsically.

As Andy defines, repped is the result of conscious contributions that are intentionally additive. By investing in positive reputation updates, whether for you or someone else, ratings rise. Relationships flourish. Trust builds. Thus, we enhance and shape an individual's online profile to a more deserving standing. Again, it's intentional.

If we do nothing and continue to post along our merry way, we become the victim of chance and circumstance. What others see and assume, the impressions that form, the opinions that arise, and the decisions they make as a result are defined for us if we do not first define and reinforce what we want them to be.

Think about it this way. When you look in the mirror, you see a reflection of who you are right now. What if you could transform that reflection each day into someone you hoped to see staring back at you? With *Repped*, we become architects of our desired reflection. If heedful, this digital reflection will ultimately work for us rather than against us. It's more than how we see ourselves, of course. It's the broad strokes we paint in addition to the fine detail that we dab to paint a portrait that helps us now and in the future.

What separates reality from aspiration are your actions and words. You earn what you deserve.

It is what we share and how we build relationships that communicate who we are, not only to those whom we know, but also those whom we wish to know as well as those who are seeking to know more about us. It takes work yes. But then again so does anything that matters in life. Where everything begins though is what's important. Most jump into online reputation management without taking what is quite honestly the most important first step…connecting the threads of who you are, your aspirations, and who it is you want others to see.

Now's the time to consider how you want to be repped. Now's the time to consider the value of online reputation management and come to terms with what you want to invest into and take out of your digital life and the digital lives of others.

Repped will help you earn digital significance. Equally, *Repped* will help you bestow significance unto others. The value you assign to engagement affects what you place and take out of this so-called digital life. The value we take away must only be surpassed by what we invest. This is the foundation for your digital legacy.

Give *repped*.

Get *repped*.

Brian Solis (@briansolis), digital analyst, anthropologist and author of *What's the Future of Business (WTF)*

INTRODUCTION

Repped (verb)—*Slang:* to add a positive reputation rating to an individual's online profile.

WHEN I SET out to write *Repped: 30 Days to a Better Online Reputation,* I endeavored to publish a book that would explain the complex world of online reputation management in a way that was both practical and easy to understand. In the six years since writing *Radically Transparent: Monitoring and Managing Reputations Online,* a lot has changed. Social media has exploded in growth and just about everyone has a Twitter account, Facebook page, or some other kind of socially connected profile. Along the way, we learned that our voices can carry much further than ever before and if an individual, business, or organization lets us down we're not afraid to complain. Loudly. Relentlessly. Fearlessly.

WHO SHOULD READ *REPPED?*

Repped is for everyone. It's for the twenty-something, fresh out of college, who realizes that his student indiscretions are hampering his job search. It's for the small business owner who's trying to build a loyal customer base that will spread the word about their love for her products. It's for the CEO of the Fortune 500 Company who's trying to rebuild a tarnished company image. And, *Repped* is for you, because whether you realize it or not, you have a reputation to protect online.

FROM REPUTATION ZERO TO HERO

Repped is written as a 30-day guide. Each chapter is a different day with a different focus. Just like the "get six-pack abs in a month" or "get ripped in 30 days" exercise videos that are so popular, *Repped* uses a similar approach. Anyone can commit to anything for just 30 days. And, if you follow through on your daily commitment, you'll see tremendous results at the end of those 30 days. Instead of building a ripped body, you'll build a rock-solid online reputation.

My goal, my hope, is that by reading *Repped* you will avoid becoming the next Anthony Weiner, Amy's Baking Company, or BP. You'll learn that a great reputation starts with a great character. You'll discover that the key to an amazing fan base is to be an amazing company. And that the only way you'll keep your reputation healthy is to keep listening to your customers, employees, coworkers, and business partners.

Just like a commitment to follow the exercise videos, building a great online reputation requires commitment on your part, but give me just 30 days and I promise you that you'll get *Repped*!

WHAT IS ONLINE REPUTATION MANAGEMENT?

"Conversations about our brand are happening everywhere, and with the Internet as the great equalizer, it doesn't matter if you know the brand intimately, or if you've had just one bad experience, it will be heard." —**Sir Richard Branson**

OVER THE NEXT 30 days, you're going to take your online reputation from zero to hero, but before you dive in to the necessary tactics, it's important to understand what online reputation management is, and isn't.

In *Radically Transparent: Monitoring and Managing Reputations Online*, my coauthor, Dr. Judy Strauss, and I spewed thousands of words in our effort to explain the concept of online reputation management. That was waaay back in 2008. Thanks to BP (oil spill), Tiger Woods (affair), and United Airlines (breaking guitars)—to name just a few—we now live in an age where most people have at least a superficial understanding of the need for online reputation management.

Just in case you call a large rock "home," and you've come out from under it just to read this book, here's a new definition of online reputation management in one sentence:

A deliberate effort to increase the number of positive Internet discussions about you, while limiting the damage of any negative ones.

Easier said than done, right?

Notice that online reputation management is not solely about manipulating what shows up on the first page of Google. Certainly, managing the search engine results is a vital part of online reputation management (we'll cover that on Day 18), but there's so much more that goes into building a great reputation, which you'll explore over the coming days.

WHY SHOULD YOU CARE?

Why should you care about your online reputation? Well, if you're a farmer in Elbonia* perhaps you don't need to worry about what people are saying about you online. And indeed, there are many individuals and companies that are blissfully unaware of their online reputation, and likely won't ever read this. For the rest of you, a single statistic might just get your attention:

90% of us trust the recommendations of others (Source: Forrester Research)

Notice, this is 90% of *anyone* else. Not just friends or family recommendations, but the recommendations of any random stranger that happens to have a computer connected to the Internet. With the rise of social media, you and I have placed our trust in the endorsements and critiques of complete and total strangers.

Is that fair?

Ask any business owner with a 1-star Yelp review, or an individual with a Klout score of 15, and you'll probably get "no" for an answer. However, just because your reputation is now being decided by anyone else but you, doesn't mean that all is lost. You're going to learn how to build, manage, monitor, and repair your online reputation. How well you succeed will be determined by one very important factor.

Your character.

HOW'S YOUR TREE?

Were he alive today, our 16th President of the United States of America, Abraham Lincoln, wouldn't make for much of a theater critic, but he might find his calling in the field of reputation management. To this day, Lincoln has one of my all-time favorite quotes on the subject:

> *"Character is like a tree and reputation like a shadow. The shadow is what we think of it; the tree is the real thing."*

No, this is not a botany lesson. Instead, it's one of the most important lessons you'll learn in your 30-day quest for a better online reputation. Your reputation will only ever be as good as your character. Sure, just as hand puppeteers can contort their fingers to display a bunny shadow on a brightly lit wall, so too could you manipulate your reputation to be something other than your true nature. But, how long would you be able to hold that pose? It wouldn't be long before your audience realizes that you're not a cute, fluffy bunny after all, just a bunch of knuckles and fingernails.

It's the same with your reputation, but that's something you can use to your advantage! As we explore different tactics for improving your online reputation, keep in mind that by simply being a better person, a better company, a better non-profit, you'll automatically start to improve your reputation.

Take care of your tree, and the shadow will take care of itself.

NOT JUST FOR COMPANY BRANDS

What reputation are you trying to improve? Your personal name? Your company brand? Your products? Your...?

As you make your way through the upcoming lessons, try not to get caught in the trap of thinking that some of the advice only applies to company reputations, or skip a recommendation that you feel is aimed at individuals. I'll be sure to point out any strategy that works better for personal versus corporate reputation management, but, for the most part, the two are interchangeable. In fact, on Day 2, you'll see just how closely personal and company reputations are entwined. What is important is that you actually do something with the lessons you learn.

DON'T WAIT FOR A REPUTATION HEART ATTACK

Fellow reputation management practitioner, Tony Wright, is constantly imploring his clients to be proactive in their reputation management. He tells them:

> "Trying to improve your online reputation during a crisis is like trying to eat healthy food during a heart attack."

The absolute worst time to try and improve your online reputation is during a full-blown reputation crisis. You need to start right now! Today is the day to start improving your online reputation, while things are calm, you have the resources and time—and you're not trying to put out reputation fires. As we work through the next 30 days, start making notes of strategies and tactics you can implement immediately. Don't think that you can put off taking control of your online reputation simply because you don't foresee any upcoming issues with your online reputation.

You don't want to be the farmer in Elbonia whose tree catches fire while he's eating a Big Mac and large fries!

TODAY'S EXERCISE

Take an honest look at your character and make a note of any changes needed before trying to improve your online reputation.

Yes, I am big fan of Scott Adams' Dilbert *comic strip.*

THERE'S NO SUCH THING AS MULTIPLE REPUTATION DISORDER

"A brand for a company is like a reputation for a person. You earn reputation by trying to do hard things well." —**Jeff Bezos**

WHEN DAN CATHY decided to verbalize his personal religious beliefs, he assumed he could do so without wearing his Chick-fil-A CEO hat. What followed were weeks of defending his position and Chick-fil-A executives desperately trying to mitigate the various verbal assaults, written diatribe, and physical store protests. While Chick-fil-A attracted an equal number of supporters—many stores saw some of their best sales in years—there was no doubt that Cathy learned a valuable lesson:

As the leader of a company, you cannot simply put a moat around your personal actions and statements.

Although Cathy later reached out to the same gay-rights activists he had scorned—and built a valuable bridge of peace—there's no doubt that a small segment of the population will forever look at Chick-fil-A's reputation a whole lot differently.

While you may expect CEOs to realize that their words and actions are intricately meshed with those of the company they run, that same accountability also runs the full stretch of the corporate ladder. During the same reputation crisis, Vante's Adam Smith decided to post a video of himself berating a Chick-fil-A employee at a Tucson drive-thru. Smith was subsequently fired from his company, while the calm, smiling, fast food worker earned a lot of kudos from Chick-fil-A for not once taking Smith's vitriol-infused bait.

YOU ARE WHAT YOU TWEET

The idea that you can't simply draw a line in the sand between your personal and business reputation is reinforced on the popular social networking site Twitter. With hundreds of millions of daily users, it doesn't take much digging around before you find examples where any line becomes blurred. Many Twitter users attempt to build their very own trench around their personal account by adding text to their Twitter bio that reads something like, "Tweets are my own views, and not that of my employer." Like me, you may read that and ask yourself, "Well of course they're your views, who else's would they be?"

Despite your best efforts to carefully craft your online reputation, as you learned on Day 1, your true character always has a way of sticking its ugly head into a conversation when you least expect it. If something similar to the following scenario hasn't happened to you yet, it will at some point.

It's late on a Friday. You're really looking forward to the weekend. The boss has been on your case all day and you have that big new client who is a royal pain in your behind. As you leave for the day, you decide to tweet your immense relief that the weekend has finally arrived. You pull up Twitter and tweet the following to your eighty-five closest friends and family:

It's the weekend! My boss can kiss my butt, and so can my new client. I plan on a very big hangover tomorrow!

Only, you forgot to log out of the company Twitter account. The one with over 35,000 followers. The one read by both your boss and your new client.

Ouch!

You can imagine the consequences, but the big question is, why tweet that at all? Ever? From any Twitter account? Even if your boss is not following you on Twitter, at some point a disgruntled coworker might show it to him or her, or a potential employer discovers it during the hiring process.

You cannot divide your personal reputation from your business one. No matter how hard you try.

YOU CAN'T KEEP IT OFFLINE

Just as you cannot keep your personal and corporate reputations from meshing, the same goes for how you act offline versus your online self. Cory Booker, former mayor of Newark, and current United States senator, almost derailed his flawless political reputation when it came to light that he was tweeting and texting with Lynsie Lee, a stripper in Portland, Oregon. Fortunately for Booker, he was single, the tweets were innocuous, and he didn't send her any photos of his private parts. Anthony Weiner, on the other hand, well, we all know how that story ended.

You simply cannot pretend to have an online reputation that is sheltered from the one of you offline. The two will always find a way to converge. It could be someone sharing a photo of you smoking a bong (Michael Phelps), or perhaps a video is posted showing one of your employees molesting pizza ingredients (Domino's Pizza). And it doesn't even have to be at the national level. You may have a great online reputation, but when people finally meet you at an industry conference, they discover that you like to drink too much and grope members of the opposite sex. Don't you think that will make it back to the online circles you've worked so hard to impress?

Whether it's something you've accidentally posted to Twitter (KitchenAid), an ill-advised statement you made when you thought no one was recording you (Mitt Romney), or just a case of being friends with someone who could tarnish your reputation (Booker), at some point you will realize that you cannot separate your online reputation from your offline actions, nor your personal opinions from those of your corporate brand.

TODAY'S EXERCISE

Check for anything on your personal social network profiles that you would never want posted to your company profile.

UNDERSTANDING YOUR ONLINE REPUTATION GOALS

"A man without a goal is like a ship without a rudder."

—**Thomas Carlyle**

BY THIS POINT, you're likely chomping at the bit, ready to start improving your online reputation, but we still have much to do. Diving right in with a reputation management campaign is probably the single biggest mistake I see made by those anxious to get *Repped*. Instead, you have to slow down and prepare a foundation that will allow you to build the best reputation possible. You wouldn't build the world's finest hotel without first drafting up the architectural plans and laying the best possible foundation. The same applies to your reputation online.

It starts by understanding your goals. What exactly are you trying to achieve? Simply declaring, "I want to build a better reputation" isn't going to cut it. We all want that! You have to be more deliberate in your efforts, and you have to follow the 3x30 rule.

THREE GOALS IN ONE

When setting goals for your online reputation campaign, it helps to divide them up into short-term, mid-term, and long-term goals. Specifically, I like to use the 3x30 approach.

30 days—What are your reputation goals for the next 30 days?

30 weeks—What are your reputation goals for the next 30 weeks?

30 months—You guessed it, what are your reputation goals for the next 30 months?

This 3x30 approach to reputation management will help you to understand your immediate needs, mid-term goals, and long-term strategy. Most of you will have some kind of short-term, urgent issue that needs to be addressed right away. The further out you plan, the more strategic and less tactical your goals will become.

Let's take a look at an example:

30-day goal—Our CEO is being attacked in a particular forum. We need to join the conversation, put out fires, correct inaccuracies, and stop the attacks from continuing.

30-week goal—We need to start positioning our CEO as a thought leader in our industry by publishing ten blog posts she has authored, building a Twitter following of at least 2,000 fans that support her, and improving what shows up on the first page in Google, when you search her name.

30-month goal—We plan to have our CEO featured as a trusted source for print and TV news outlets. All negative search engine results will be pushed beyond the first three pages and she will speak at three conferences throughout the year.

These goals won't be set in stone. Every 30 days you'll need to come up with a revised 30-day goal, which may also result in a change for your 30-week and 30-month goals. The key is to have a plan in place from the outset and commit to it for 30 days. After that, reevaluate, repeat if necessary, and adapt as you do, or do not, make progress.

BENCHMARK YOUR ONLINE REPUTATION

Once you've realized your 3x30 goals, you will need to take a benchmark reading of your online reputation. If your 30-day goal were to improve the sentiment towards your CEO in a particular forum, then you would start by measuring the number of positive mentions in that forum, versus any negative ones. Thirty days from now, measure the same numbers and see if you've pushed the reputation needle in the right direction.

If you're trying to increase the number of Facebook fans you have, then that's an easy number to calculate over the next 30 days. If your goal is to improve your influence and reach on Twitter, measuring your Klout.com score makes that task equally easy to complete. What else might you benchmark? Depending on the goals you've set forth, you could measure any of the following:

- Your average review rating on sites such as Amazon, Yelp, or TripAdvisor.
- The amount of positive results on the first page of Google.
- The number of backlinks pointing to your website.
- The number of times your reputation is mentioned on a forum or message board.
- The amount of complaints received by your customer service team.

- The percentage of employees who approve of your CEO on Glassdoor.

THE ONE GOAL WE ALL SHARE

As you can see, there are a number of different ways to measure the success of your online reputation campaign. That said, for the most part, there's a common goal that unites us all. Money. While the social media gurus will tell you that your main goal should be to have a campfire singsong with your fans and detractors, it's okay to admit that you'd like to make some money along the way. Sure, we all want to be liked, loved, cherished, or valued, but the main reason for improving your online reputation is that it increases your ability to generate more income.

A positive reputation leads to a higher salary, greater corporate revenues, or increases in online donations. We don't have to be ashamed of ourselves for having that goal. Money is not the root of all evil; it's what you do with it, when you get it, that cause many to fall.

When you draw up the goals for your online reputation, be honest with yourself about what it is you wish to achieve. Having more Facebook fans is not a worthy goal, unless you know what benefits those fans will actually bring you.

TODAY'S EXERCISE

Outline your 3x30 goals and benchmark your reputation so you can measure your future success.

THE REPUTATION SIX

"The blaze of reputation cannot be blown out, but it often dies in the socket; a very few names may be considered as perpetual lamps that shine unconsumed." —**Samuel Johnson**

NOW THAT I have you convinced that you only have one reputation, I'm going to thoroughly confuse you by walking you through how to identify all of the reputations that may require your focus over the next 30 days.

Before you feel cheated, allow me to explain.

It is true that as "Andy Beal" I have the same reputation online as I do offline, and the same one whether I'm tweeting for myself, or on behalf of my company. We're not moving away from that principle. However, what I do want you to understand is that you have many more reputations than just your personal name, or the name of your company.

If you want to get *Repped*, then you need to make sure that every possible reputation under your control looks as good as possible.

After all, you wouldn't work out for 30 days to get rock solid abs without also working on your arms, legs, shoulders, etc. With that in mind, let's look at the six reputations that most of you will need to nurture and protect.

YOUR PERSONAL NAME

Yes, we've covered this in Day 3. However, you should consider whether you have variations of your name which you need to manage. If your name is John Smith, but you also go by Johnny Smith, then you either need to just pick one variation and stick with it, or concede that you now have two different personal brands to manage. For me, I go by Andy Beal 100% of the time—unless I'm sitting down for dinner with my mother, who insists on calling me Andrew.

YOUR NICKNAMES

Let's face it, by the time you finally joined the latest social media network, the chances are you weren't able to grab your real name as your username. Instead, you were forced to use a nickname—and hopefully you didn't choose "fluffybunny247" because that presents a whole new level of reputation management.

In addition, back before online reputation management became so vital, many folks decided to use nicknames for all of their online accounts. For example, Internet marketing mastermind Michael Gray is known as "Graywolf" in all of the industry circles that matter to him. Now he has to pay close attention to the reputation of both his real name, and his nickname.

YOUR COMPANY NAME

Your personal brand and your company brand are intrinsically linked; you learned that on Day 3. It therefore makes sense to ensure that your company reputation is presented as positively as possible. Just as with your personal name, you may not be able to rely on sole management of your official company name. For example, the pharmaceutical giant GlaxoSmithKline is also known as Glaxo, GSK, and by legacy names such as Glaxo Wellcome and Smithkline Beecham.

YOUR PRODUCT/SERVICE NAMES

Most small and medium-sized businesses won't have an array of product or service names to worry about, but if you're Apple, Google, or GlaxoSmithKline, then you may have dozens, nay hundreds, of products to protect from reputation attacks. While it may not be practical to monitor and manage the reputations of all of your products, you certainly should pay attention to those that generate the most revenue and kudos for you.

YOUR CEO AND OTHER EXECUTIVES

I once worked for a company where the CEO kept a very low profile and let others handle all public announcements and speaking engagements. As you can imagine, if he was discussed online, it was generally not anything that was planned. Consequently, we kept a watchful eye for any discussions that included his name.

You may be the CEO, so you can obviously skip this step. If not, then you will want to make sure you protect the reputation of your CEO, C-level executives, and any other prominent employees. For example, Google's Matt Cutts is not part of the search engine's C-suite, but he is the spokesperson for all things related to the company's algorithm and spam-fighting efforts. If you were managing the online reputation for Google, Cutts would be high on your list of reputations to monitor and manage.

YOUR MARKETING MESSAGES

It's the Real Thing.
Because You're Worth It.
We Try Harder.

You probably recognize at least one of the above marketing slogans. Coca-Cola, L'Oreal, and Avis have all spent a lot of time and money to ensure that their messages are stored away tightly in the recesses of your brain. Knowing where, when, and how each message is shared on the web is a priority for each of these corporate giants. Likewise, if you have a marketing message, tagline, or other slogan that is tied to your brand, you should include it in your online reputation management efforts.

IT'S TIME TO START LISTENING

As you get ready to move into Day 5 of *Repped*, you now have an understanding of all the reputations that are important to you. The next step is to start monitoring as many online conversations about these reputations as you possibly can. If you don't know what's being said, you won't know the work needed in order to improve sentiment towards each reputation. Onward!

TODAY'S EXERCISE

Using the first six outlined points, make a list of all the reputations you need to focus on over the next 30 days.

ACTIVELY LISTEN

"To listen well, is as powerful a means of influence as to talk well, and is as essential to all true conversation." —**Chinese Proverb**

NOW THAT YOU understand the different reputations that will need your focus over the coming weeks and months, it's time to figure out where exactly those reputations are being discussed. Hopefully, you already have at least a vague idea of the different blogs, networks, forums, and other online watercoolers where your customers, partners, and industry peers tend to hang out. If not, don't panic. I'm going to walk you through a simple process to determine where your reputations are being discussed and how best to join these conversations.

IT ALL STARTS WITH GOOGLE

Let's be honest, while there are many moving parts to online reputation management, just about everything centers around

Google. So that's where you'll start with your online listening. Now, before I have you head over to Google.com and start searching your various reputations, there's something important you need to know.

Google is biased.

Not a shock, I know, but for the most part that's not a bad thing. In fact, just about any time you search for something on Google, the search engine giant will customize results with just enough personalization that it hopes you're more likely to find something that appeals to you. That kind of bias is normally beneficial, but for your research, you want to strip out that bias. It doesn't help you if Google shows you a website or social network that it knows you like or frequent a lot. You're trying to find the ones that your customers, partners, and other reputation stakeholders use.

So, how do you strip out that bias? The best solution is to fire up Google's Chrome browser and open an Incognito Tab. When you do, you'll see this message:

*You've gone incognito. Pages you view in this window won't appear in your browser history or search history, and they won't leave other traces, like cookies, on your computer after you close **all** open incognito windows. Any files you download or bookmarks you create will be preserved, however.*

When you search while incognito, Google doesn't know all of your prior preferences and you are much more likely to get an unbiased view of the web.

Now that you're no longer seeing the results that Google thinks you will prefer, you can start searching for your reputations and discover which social networks, forums, and blogs tend to show up in the first twenty to thirty results. Make a note of any that appear to be hubs for potential or existing customers to hang out. You'll use this list again on Day 6.

ANALYZE YOUR ANALYTICS

The next step in listening is to take a look at the web analytics software you use to track all visitors to your site. Google Analytics (I told you everything revolves around Google) is a robust, free solution, but any web analytics vendor is fine for this task.

Once you have your web analytics in front of you, set the date criteria for the past six months or so, and in particular, drill down to the list of websites that refer traffic to your own site. If you don't have a website, you can skip this step (you'll learn later on that there are many reputation benefits to owning your own website).

With the list of referring sites in front of you, make a note of any that send a sizeable chunk of visitors to your website. There's a reason why those sites are sending you traffic and we need to start monitoring them to see if those reasons are favorable to your reputation or not.

MANUAL MONITORING

Now that you've compiled a list from both Google and your web analytics, you have a seed list of websites that you should monitor on a regular basis. You can either manually visit these sites each day and check for any new mentions of your reputation, or you can find an automated solution that will check them for you.

AUTOMATE YOUR ONLINE MONITORING

The reason you just went through the above steps is that far too many people sign up for a social media monitoring software solution without having any idea of what exactly it is they need to monitor. Now that you have your seed list, you have a better understanding of whether you need a solution that monitors forums, review sites, Twitter, Facebook, or perhaps some specific industry-focused site, such as TripAdvisor.

With that knowledge, you can research which of the three different types of social media monitoring tools best fit your needs. Let's take a look at them:

Free—Free tools such as Google Alerts or Social Mention have one great advantage going for them: they are free. Unfortunately, that typically comes with a lot of limitations and you may find that any free monitoring tool lacks the features you're looking for, or doesn't have the coverage you need. Still, for the majority of you, a free tool will be sufficient for your monitoring needs.

Self-Service—The limitations of the many free tools is the very reason I decided to launch Trackur.com in 2008. For less than a the price of a latte a day, Trackur provides broad coverage of the Internet, lets you measure influence and sentiment, and will send you alerts via RSS or e-mail. If you don't have deep pockets, and are willing to roll up your sleeves, a self-service monitoring solution such as Trackur is a great choice.

Full-Service—If you have the budget, or perhaps don't have the time, you can use a solution such as SAS's Social Media Analytics or salesforce.com's Marketing Cloud (formerly Radian6). With a full-service monitoring solution, you'll receive robust social media analytics, full support from their expert staff, and a lighter wallet.

MORE THAN JUST HEARING

The biggest mistake you could make at this point is to simply listen. Normal listening is no better than hearing. You hear the conversation, but you do nothing with the information. Instead you need to actively listen to what is being said about your reputation.

Wikipedia defines active listening as follows:

Active listening is a communication technique used in counseling, training and conflict resolution, which requires the listener to feed back what they hear to the speaker, by way of re-stating or paraphrasing what they have heard in their own words, to confirm what they have heard and moreover, to confirm the understanding of both parties.

In other words, demonstrate to those talking about your reputation that you care about what they say, by doing something about the feedback they've provided.

This would be a good time to think about who will be responsible for listening to the online conversations and then making sure any feedback is acted upon. If you're managing your own personal reputation, congratulations, the job is yours! If you're part of a larger organization, then you'll initially assign this role to someone who already has similar responsibilities and then eventually create a full-time position.

FINDING YOUR CENTERS OF INFLUENCE

Let's recap.

You've used Google and your web analytics to seed the list of websites that are already discussing your reputation. You've also chosen a social media monitoring solution that will help you to automate the process of identifying any new conversations. Lastly, you, or someone on your team, have committed to actively listen to those conversations.

You're almost ready to start joining these reputation discussions. Before you do, you need to identify the rules of engagement for the online networks and communities you are about to join. You need to understand your reputation's centers of influence.

TODAY'S EXERCISE

If you do nothing else today, head to google.com/alerts or trackur.com to set up your social media monitoring

.

FINDING YOUR CENTERS OF INFLUENCE

"You have to make sure you start to influence the customer early on. You have to outthink and outsmart your competitors."—**Lee Cooper**

WITH A BETTER understanding of where your reputation is being discussed, you can start to short-list those conversations that you wish to join. While you should monitor as many news sites, blogs, and social networks as you possibly can—you never know where you may be discussed—it would be impractical to actively engage and build your online reputation everywhere your customers might hang out. Instead, you need to focus on your reputation's "Centers of Influence." Where is it that your stakeholders hang out?

WHO HAS A SAY IN YOUR REPUTATION?

This is an appropriate point to introduce you to the term *stakeholders*. While it's easy to focus all of your attention on your customers, potential or existing, they make up only a small subset of those that are discussing your online reputation. Along with their thoughts and opinions, you also need to consider the following:

Employees—Unless you work for some super-secret government agency, your employees and coworkers will at some point publicly share their thoughts about you.

Business partners—Those who purchase products from you or those who provide you with services and solutions, are also likely to mention your brand online.

Journalists—Hopefully if a mainstream news publication talks about your reputation, it will be a good thing, but they may also dig up some of your skeletons.

Bloggers—The lines are blurring between journalists and bloggers, but bloggers often don't have to check facts or seek you out for a quote before publishing their opinion about you.

Industry influencers—Thanks to social networks such as Twitter, industry influencers can reach hundreds of thousands of people, and influence their opinion on a company or individual, in less than 140 characters!

Trolls—They live under the bridges of the Internet. They either don't like you specifically, or they just love to cause havoc indiscriminately.

Together with your customers, they make up the stakeholders in your online reputation. Where they hang out will influence where you should focus your efforts to get *Repped.*

STALKING, THE NON-CREEPY WAY

Now that you know who's talking about you, and where they tend to hang out, it's time to start learning the rules of engagement. Each blog, forum, or social network will have its own rules of the game. Before you join the conversation, you need to learn those rules. You wouldn't ever barge into a cocktail party and start talking about yourself and your interests. The same goes for your centers of influence.

To be effective in your efforts to build a better reputation, you should spend some time not just listening for conversations about your brand, but also stalking those that host them. Now, I would hate to see any of you hit with a restraining order, so let's talk a little about how to stalk on the Internet. What I am proposing is you take time to observe the rules of engagement—written or implied—for any of your centers of influence. Here are some examples of how to do just that.

BLOGS

Once you've identified bloggers who are influential in your industry, then you should start reading their posts. Get to know them. What do they like to write about? What do they hate to see in a company? Which brands are they passionate about? Subscribe to their blog posts using either e-mail or RSS and perhaps even take the time to leave a comment or two. Not only will you get a better idea of how to stay on their radar, but you'll also learn how to avoid their wrath.

FORUMS

The great thing about a forum or message board is that you can set up a profile and just lurk. Lurking is one of the great pastimes of many forum members. You can just read what others have to say, without feeling the need to chime in with your own two cents. Take time to read the forum rules and then watch how members interact with each other. Which threads tend to attract the most positive attention? Which topics quickly result in a full on flame attack? Remember, we're just stalking at this point. Engagement comes later.

TWITTER

Twitter really only has one hard and fast rule. You can't publish anything longer than 140 characters. Everything else is pretty much subjective and open to interpretation. What may be acceptable in one industry would be frowned upon in another. Start following those that are already talking about your brand and use Followerwonk.com to find influential Twitter users in your industry.

FACEBOOK

Facebook is the leading social network for connecting with friends, family, and brands that you are passionate about. I mention Facebook specifically, but your reputation's center of influence could just as easily be Google+ or Instagram. Again, start following those that are influential in your particular industry or have previously discussed your reputation. Pay attention to not only what they share, but also the comments that are left by others. With these social communities, it's the author of a post who steers the bus, but it's the fans who provide the fuel.

YOU CAN'T BE EVERYWHERE

At this point, you've identified your centers of influence and are getting to know the rules of engagement. Don't feel pressure to manage your online reputation on every single blog or in every single social network. You don't have the time. Instead, you're going to be proactive in managing your reputation in a handful of these centers of influence and reactive to any discussions that come up elsewhere.

That said, just because you can't single-handedly maintain an active role in all of these online hangouts, doesn't mean they can go completely ignored. There is a way to expand your reputation's reach and it happens with the help of your friends, family, and employees. That's your focus for Day 7.

TODAY'S EXERCISE

Identify where your stakeholders are hanging out online and start doing the same.

EMPOWERING OTHERS

"Ask not what your country can do for you, but what you can do for your country." —**John F. Kennedy**

I HAVE GOOD news and bad news about your online reputation. The good news is, you don't have to do this on your own. Your friends, family, and coworkers can just as easily influence how others perceive your reputation. The bad news is, your friends, family, and coworkers can just as easily influence how others perceive your reputation.

Okay, perhaps you saw that coming, but in this chapter you're going to focus your efforts to get *Repped* by making sure that those around you are singing from the same song sheet, and not inadvertently undermining your online reputation.

FIRM BUT FAIR

There's a reason why mattress stores suggest you change your mattress every ten years. It's because they know it takes at least that long for you to forget just how much of a chore it is to shop for a mattress. My wife and I had put off this task for too long and finally gave up our procrastination and started shopping for a mattress.

Mattress shopping is a very subjective process. The reputation of a mattress store is easily influenced by not just the actual mattress brand purchased, but also by the staff that sell you the mattress. After visiting a number of well-known mattress chains, we found Mike at our local Mattress Firm store.

Mike wasn't pushy. He didn't pressure us. He, can you believe this, actually listened to our needs and our feedback. Mike did a fantastic job of helping us find the perfect mattress for my wife and me.

Except it wasn't.

After just a few nights of sleeping on our new mattress, we realized that it was far too soft for us. Fortunately, Mike was not only sympathetic, but he made good on his company's 100-day comfort guarantee and readily agreed to switch out the mattress for a new one. With a better idea of our sleep preferences, Mike helped us find our new perfect mattress—a rather pricey Tempur-Pedic memory foam mattress with an adjustable base and special cooling technology!

Yeah, that mattress didn't work out for us either.

At this point I thought Mike might actually duck under his desk as he saw us approach his store for the third time, but he welcomed us back with a smile and sincere desire to help us find the perfect mattress. Another round of questions and testing, and we finally decided on a mattress aptly named "Joy."

Success!

What Mike didn't know was that I had read many negative online reviews about the Mattress Firm prior to our hunt for a perfect night's sleep. I was reluctant to even shop at the store. Despite bringing all of my prejudices with me, Mike was able to demonstrate that a single employee could define how I perceived the company's reputation.

Mike *was* the Mattress Firm's reputation.

EMPOWER, DON'T RESTRAIN

How do you create an army of "Mikes" for your brand?

You build a better reputation by empowering your employees to do as much as they possibly can to ensure the happiness of your customers. That's it! No social media handbooks, no corporate policies. You place trust in your employees and give them the opportunity to shine.

At this point, you're probably recalling the many different reputation scandals that were caused by rogue employees. Abusive tweets. Vulgar videos. Distasteful photos. There are many examples where a popular brand had its online reputation tarnished by the actions of one bad employee. The answer to that is not found in restrictive policies or complex guidelines. Those merely focus on preventing the symptoms; they do nothing to address the root problem: you need to hire better employees.

Hire employees that really want the job. Hire those that are passionate about your industry. Hire those that love what you do and will take a social media bullet to defend your online reputation. Then, empower them. Here's how:

Your story—Tell them about your company's story. Why was it started? What goals (the ones you came up with on Day 3) does it hope to achieve?

Your message—What's the driving message for your brand? For what ideal does it wish to be known?

Your fears—What's your biggest reputation fear? Let your employees know the things that keep you awake at night. With this knowledge, they'll know what conversations to avoid and when to alert you to something that might hurt your reputation.

Your support—Tell them that you have their back. For example, at Trackur we don't offer customer refunds for payments already collected. You can cancel at any time, so we feel it only fair if you make a payment, you should honor it. That said, we make exceptions all the time, based on individual circumstances, and have yet to question any employee's decision to refund a customer's payment.

If you want your employees to help you build a better reputation, let them know how they can best do that.

AMBITION TRUMPS ALTRUISM

If you've hired the right people, then you should find that they quickly become just as passionate about your reputation as you. However, that doesn't mean you shouldn't point out the benefits that your staff will receive when they work to improve your online reputation. Altruism will motivate them to do only so much. Ambition is the catalyst that will fuel their desire to make your company better.

When you educate and empower your employees, they quickly see that a company with great products, happy customers, and a positive reputation leads to higher salaries, better working conditions, and greater opportunities for promotion. When your employees become part of your online reputation, they also become more valuable to your company. They help grow your company's reputation while simultaneously growing their own. After working many years to demonstrate that Google had a reputation for great web services, Marissa Mayer had built an equally valuable personal reputation—one she carried with her when she accepted the role of CEO at rival Yahoo.

BRAND AMBASSADORS

It's easy to focus this lesson on empowering employees at your company, but what if you don't have a company? What if you're the only employee? What if you're merely trying to improve your personal reputation, how does all of this apply to you?

Quite simply, everything can apply, even if you don't have employees. An employee is just one of the many brand ambassadors for your reputation. If you're a non-profit, then supplement the word employee with volunteer. When they call someone for a donation, do they know your organization's message? For individual reputation management, take the above advice and apply it to your friends or family. Let them know that what they post to your Facebook wall, or publish to Flickr, can affect your online reputation. Do they know the reputation you're trying to build for yourself?

No matter whether you're an individual, small business, or Fortune 500, you're going to need help with your efforts to build a better online reputation, and tomorrow we'll start doing just that!

TODAY'S EXERCISE

Write down your story, message, and fears and share them with your employees, friends, and family.

SETTING UP AND BUILDING YOUR SOCIAL MEDIA PROFILES

"I look at the blog just as I look at any other product." —**Bob Parsons**

IF YOU'RE THE kind of person who likes to roll up your sleeves and just get the job done, then you're going to enjoy Day 8 of *Repped*. Today, you're going to take your first steps to building a better reputation.

Now that you've discovered your centers of influence, it's time to discover your voice. It's time to start building an audience of influencers that will help you improve your online reputation and achieve your goals.

HELLO, MY NAME IS...

Choosing the right name can make or break your reputation management efforts. For your blog, the name you use in your title is not as important as the name you select for your URL. You may be tempted to head over to GoDaddy.com or some other domain registrar, and register something inspiring or trendy, such as ThoughtsonFire.com or DriventoDeliver.com. Unfortunately, neither mentions your name, so neither is going to do much to help you improve your online reputation.

For individuals, you would be much better off selecting a domain name that matches your real name. For example, I have two personal blogs. One at AndyBeal.com and the other at AndyBeal.me. Both include my real name, so both help me with my reputation efforts, especially when it comes to controlling what shows up in Google and other search engines.

For corporations and other organizations, my advice is to locate your blog in a sub-directory or sub-folder of your existing branded site. Using mycompany.com/blog or blog.myorganization.org allows you to piggyback off your existing search engine credibility and saves you a few bucks in domain name registration fees in the process!

For your social networking profiles, you should use the name that matches the reputation you're trying to improve. Knowem.com offers a free tool that will allow you to see if your desired profile name is available across dozens of different social networking sites. For a small fee, it will also register and complete your social networking profiles for you.

POTENTIAL NAMING CHALLENGES

When checking for the availability of your desired profile name, you may discover that it's already registered.

Don't panic!

There's a good chance that you previously registered the profile, but it was back when Twitter's fail whale was just a minnow. Search through your e-mail for the registration confirmation, or ask the social network to re-send you your password and see if the e-mail comes to you. If not, then go ahead, you can panic a little, but all is not lost.

If your preferred username is not available, you have a couple of choices. First, if you hold a registered trademark for the name, you can often submit supporting documentation and request that the existing username be handed over to you. This happened to us at Trackur when we finally decided to join Pinterest and pin our blog posts and other interesting news. Someone had already registered the Trackur username, which prevented us from registering it. A couple of weeks after submitting a trademark claim form to Pinterest, the username was handed over to us.

If you don't have that option-say you're trying to register something common such as "JohnSmith" or "RegencyRealEstate"—then you're going to have to get a little creative. Just a little, though. Now is not the time to abandon your real name in favor of something nondescript or cute. Instead, try using variations of your desired name. Use something that includes your name alongside a descriptor.

For example, "JohnSmithAttorney" or "RegencyRealEstateRaleigh."

BUILDING YOUR AUDIENCE

Once you have your blog and social networking profiles up and running, it's time to decide which of those to invest in. I say "invest" because simply setting up a blog or Twitter account is not going to help you to improve your online reputation. You have to build it out with interesting and valuable content, and grow and nurture your audience.

Why should someone read, follow, like, share, or retweet you? For some of you, publishing a blog or posting a tweet will involve the bare minimum of effort. You'll share a few updates, just enough to get the attention of Google, then never touch it again. You'll see your content rise to the first ten results in the search engines, be content with your reputation efforts, and take your foot off the gas. The problem with this approach is that you're assuming that your reputation is static, Google's algorithm never changes, and that you can just fire and forget.

Sorry, that's just wishful thinking.

Your online reputation is always changing, sometimes growing, sometimes shrinking. Merely posting a couple of items and calling it a job well done is naive at best, and risky at worst. By continuing to share valuable and insightful blog posts, tweets, and updates, you grow your audience. You nurture your centers of influence.

SPREAD YOURSELF AROUND

Before you reach for a brown paper bag, there's no need to hyperventilate at the thought of growing and managing all possible social networking profiles on the web. Remember, you should focus your efforts on your centers of influence. This means investing time and effort only in those networks where you know your stakeholders tend to hang out. For many of you, your blog, Twitter, Facebook, and LinkedIn will make up the four pillars of your online reputation management efforts. That means that while you can't completely ignore secondary social networks such as Instagram, Tumblr, or Pinterest, you also don't have to spend all of your extra time growing and nurturing those communities.

Whichever social networks you decide require your focus, you will need to make sure that your pithy comments, insightful posts, and hilarious updates don't go unnoticed. You can do that by:

Linking to them – From your corporate or personal website, make sure you link to your blog and social networking profiles.

E-mail signature – Have all of your employees include a link to your blog or social profile in the signature of their e-mails.

Your printed materials – Your business cards, direct mail, and brochures should all include links to your blog and social networking profiles. Don't just say "Find us on Facebook." Instead, include the full link to your Facebook profile, so they don't have to find you!

Your TV and Radio ads – If you have the budget to run radio or TV ads, then include your social networking profiles. If someone is a fan of your brand, let them know where to connect with you.

This is not an exhaustive list. It serves as a reminder that "if you build it, they will come" only applies to baseball fields. For your blog and social profiles, you're going to have to work hard to attract attention. The best way to do that is to be proactive in your efforts. However, there is a way to set up your social profiles and blog so that they grow your audience while you sleep, but we'll get to that tomorrow.

TODAY'S EXERCISE

Register your username at all the social networks that match your centers of influence.

KEEPING THE SEARCH ENGINE SPIDERS HAPPY

"If it isn't on Google, it doesn't exist." —**Jimmy Wales**

1,873,910,000,000.

THAT'S A BIG number. What does it represent? It's the estimated number of search queries that happen on Google each year. Let me put that number into perspective for you:

If you conducted one search every second, it would take you nearly 60,000 years to match the same number of searches Google sees annually.

The goal today is to highlight the important role that Google plays in your efforts to build a better online reputation. And if the sheer number of searches doesn't get your attention, then perhaps this statistic will:

89% of consumers surveyed use Internet search engines to make purchasing decisions (source: 2012 Digital Influence Index).

In the absence of anything positive that you have published, Google will fill the void with search results that could quickly damage your online reputation. That should send a chill down your spine, but there is good news. Google is not biased. It is sentiment-agnostic. It merely wants to display the most relevant results for the searcher's query, regardless of whether they are positive or negative.

Unfortunately, despite all of the PhDs who tirelessly work to improve Google's algorithm, the search engine's spider is still rather stupid—and that's something you can use to your advantage!

SEARCH ENGINE REPUTATION MANAGEMENT

Pure search engine optimization (SEO) is a terrifically complex process. If you want your web page to show up in the first ten results for the keyword "Seattle real estate" you have to first outsmart Google's algorithm and then you have to outmaneuver all of the other websites that are vying to rank for the same keyword. Fortunately, your reputation management strategy is focused on ranking for your brand name or your personal name, neither of which face much competition. For the most part, you're not going to find a lot of other websites actively trying to rank for your name.

That doesn't mean that your search engine reputation management (SERM) efforts will be without challenge. While you may not be vying to get your web page to #1 on Google or Bing for a competitive keyword, you are trying to take control of the first ten results that show up when someone searches your name. Not as much competition, but ten times the number of pages to optimize!

Fortunately, on Day 8, you started building out your web pages and social networking profiles and ensured that each included your personal name or that of your company. That's a great foundation from which to build out web content that will show up at the top of Google, crowd out any negative pages, and improve your online reputation.

NAMING YOUR URLS

When you set up a social media profile, you will likely be assigned a URL that looks like this:

https://plus.google.com/118143096363038158137

You probably have no clue as to the owner of that Google+ profile. Unless you took a wild guess that it was mine, you likely had to type the link into your browser in order to discover the owner. The search engines have the same problem.

Contrast the above with the following:

https://plus.google.com/+AndyBeal1

A little easier, huh?

The point I am making is that, wherever possible, you should customize your social media profile URLs so that they include your name. By doing so, you send an early signal to the search engines that the URL is relevant to you, and isn't just a bunch of random numbers. Facebook, Twitter, LinkedIn, Flickr, and Pinterest are just a few examples of social networks that will let you customize your profile URL.

ABOUT WHOM?

The same approach should be taken with any web page that you are using for reputation management purposes. I make this distinction because I am not advocating that all of your web pages include your name in the URL, but if they are being optimized, or built, to help improve your online reputation, you should include your personal or company name.

The most obvious place to do that, but strangely the one place where many of us ignore this tactic, is with our About Us page. There are almost 7 million URLs in Google's index that have "about-us" in their page name. That's 7 million wasted opportunities. You're not going to make the same mistake. For any page that you build from scratch (don't change existing pages unless you know what "301" means), you're going to use "about-name" or "about-companyname" in the URL for your About Us page.

While you're at it, the visible headline you use on that page? Don't use "About Us" as the text; instead use "About Name" or "About Company Name." This is another signal to Google that the page is relevant enough to show in the top ten of its search results.

IMAGES ARE VALUABLE TOO

The same approach should be taken for naming images or videos that you upload to the web. It's so easy to focus all of your efforts on what web pages show up when someone Googles your name that you can quickly forget images and videos are also pervasive in the search results.

The same approach to naming your web pages and social profiles should also be applied to your images and videos. Before uploading and publishing photos or movies, you should take the time to optimize the URLs for each. The image *firstname-lastname.jpg* will more likely match against a search for your name, than one named *DSC15673.jpg*.

WHY I'M ANTI PRONOUN

The last tip for today will further help your web pages and social profiles to show up higher in the search results. My recommendation is to ditch pronouns and instead make a concerted effort to write your bios in the third person.

It may feel strange at first, but recall that the search engines are not very smart. They need as many signals as possible to inform them that the page they are crawling is relevant enough to show up when someone searches your name. When you complete profiles and bios in the first person—"I am a cosmetic surgeon in San Francisco"—you do little to instruct Google that the page is about you. Instead, writing bios in the third person—"Jane Smith is a cosmetic surgeon in San Francisco"—provides the search engine spiders with a clear indication that the content is relevant to you.

WHY GO TO ALL OF THIS TROUBLE?

It takes a lot of hard work to get your stakeholders to notice and engage with your web pages and social media profiles. These small optimization tweaks are not a magic bullet in and of themselves, but combined with your efforts to promote your online reputation, they'll contribute their share and help your stakeholders discover your voice.

Oh yes, your voice. Let's talk about that next.

TODAY'S EXERCISE

Check each of your profile bios and your About Us page and see if you need to optimize in the third person.

CONGRUENCE IS KEY TO A SOLID ONLINE REPUTATION

"The way to gain good reputation is to endeavor to be what you desire to appear." —**Socrates**

IT'S ONE THING to know your goals, your reputations, and your centers of influence, but do you know what you desire to appear? Put differently, does your online reputation have a clear and distinct voice? Not literally, although it would be nice if Morgan Freeman lent his voice to your reputation efforts, but if you were to ask your stakeholders to describe your brand, how would they describe it?

It's vital to decide how you plan to present your reputation to your stakeholders, and to then actually stick to that plan. Too many reputations are unnecessarily muddled because there's no congruence in the tone of voice used across different online and offline channels.

FINDING YOUR VOICE

If you look like a duck and quack like a duck, then you'll always have a reputation for being a duck. However, you can decide what type of duck you portray. Daffy, Donald, and Howard are all ducks, but each has a distinct personality, a different style. If you're a bank, then you need to instill trust, security, and responsibility, but the way Wells Fargo goes about that task is completely different to Ally Bank.

So, how do you find your reputation's style? Its voice? It all goes back to your character. However you decide to portray your reputation online, it shouldn't be so far removed from your character that you essentially have to fake it each and every day. It should be something that is authentic and easy to maintain, while at the same time appealing enough to attract new customers and other stakeholders.

BUILD A REPUTATION STYLE GUIDE

Until you become comfortable with your reputation's voice, you should probably jot down some notes on how you do, and do not, wish to come across in your social media activities. Branding executives often create a style guide that documents every detail of how best to use the company's logo. Its precise height and width proportions. Not just the color, but the exact pantone or hexadecimal notation is documented. The style guide is especially important during the launch or redesign of a logo, but over time is less relied upon as the company becomes familiar with its own identity. In a similar manner, you should create your reputation's style guide.

Some things to consider for your reputation style guide:

- How do we naturally communicate with our stakeholders?
- What do our stakeholders expect from us?
- What's the typical demographic we're trying to reach?
- Are we family friendly, or are we edgier than that?
- Will we engage in conversations about politics or religion?
- Do we have any legal or industry restrictions on what we can or cannot say?

Creating a style guide for your online reputation will help solidify the voice you will use in your blog, in social media, and in more formal communications such as your press releases. Even if you never look at it again, the mere act of creating it will help you to better understand how you wish to appear online.

YOUR TWITTERVATOR PITCH

Now that you have a better understanding of how you wish to portray yourself online, it's time to craft your first Twittervator pitch. Why yes, I did just totally make up that word. Rename it if you wish, but the key is to take the traditional elevator pitch—an explanation of who you are, so succinct, you could share it in a thirty-second elevator ride—and turn it into something you can use online. Twitter allows you to use only 140 characters in each tweet, teaching you to get your message across in just a sentence or two. Therefore, it makes sense to combine your elevator pitch with Twitter's restrictions. Draft up different ways of describing yourself in just 140 characters and then pick the one you feel best fits your voice and your goals. And yes, it's okay if you have to stretch it to 160 characters.

BE CONGRUENT

Once you have your Twittervator pitch—I promise, that is the last time I will use that word today—you can start building out your online profiles using it and your reputation style guide. I don't just mean take your pitch and plaster it across your blog and social media channels. Instead, use it as a starting point to build congruence in your online reputation efforts. The avatar you use, your cover photo, your bio, your initial posts: they should all tie back to your pitch.

This deliberate effort to be congruent will ensure that your stakeholders receive a consistent experience with your reputation, no matter where they connect with you. Certainly, you should adapt it slightly to suit the nuances of each channel—you may be slightly more whimsical on Pinterest than you are on LinkedIn—but don't stray too far from your reputation's style guide. You have many different centers of influence and while you need to appeal to each audience, you should do so by remaining authentic.

AVOID THE QUICK THRILL

In your efforts to be authentic, to follow your reputation style guide, you will likely get frustrated that things are not growing quickly enough. You look around the web and you see that GoPro is growing its audience rapidly by posting cool videos, or that George Takei is insanely popular because he's always posting humorous cartoons and photos. As you see your own audience grow at a painfully slow pace, you may be tempted to post that salacious photo or share that popular meme. Don't! Seriously, just don't do it. Unless that is the reputation that you wish to build, then don't take shortcuts in an effort to build an audience quickly. All you will accomplish is the fleeting attention of a transient audience with no interest in buying your product, using your service, or employing you.

You don't have to share sensational content that has little benefit to the reputation you are trying to build. Instead, you can build your own amazing content. Content that will not just attract attention, but the attention of those in your centers of influence. Those that will help you meet your reputation goals.

On Day 11 you'll learn how.

TODAY'S EXERCISE

Create a reputation style guide, then use it to help craft your own Twittervator pitch. Darn it. I used that word again when I said I wouldn't. Sorry.

CREATE AMAZING CONTENT

"Creating something is only half the battle. The other half is finding people who care about it." —**Ramsey Isler**

ACHIEVING TWENTY MILLION video views on YouTube is no easy task. It's even more difficult if you're a North American discount store and not Justin Bieber or Miley Cyrus. And if your discount store isn't named either Walmart or Target, then getting twenty million people to watch your video is somewhat incredible. To achieve something this amazing, you have to create something amazing and that is exactly what Kmart did with its "Ship My Pants" ad campaign.

The play on words brought out the twelve-year-old kid in all of us and we gladly tweeted, liked, and shared Kmart's attempt to gain attention. That a fifty-year-old company, which could never quite match the presence of Walmart or the image of Target, made the video fueled our amazement. Kmart had found a formula that captured our attention and allowed it to stand out from the crowd. It had gone beyond creating something that was merely "good."

BE BETTER THAN GOOD

How many times have you heard an Internet marketing expert say that the key to getting more traffic, fans, or links is to "create good content"? Oh, really? Because I'm sure you wake up each morning thinking "today, I plan to create something really awful." No, I didn't think so. The problem is that good content is no longer good enough. Everyone is creating good content these days. You have to step it up to "amazing content."

Creating something amazing is not going to be easy. If it were, then everyone would be doing it and then I'd have to tell you to create "outstanding content" instead. Amazing content takes planning. It takes time. And it may take money. If you're fortunate, you'll create something amazing once a month. Let me rephrase that. You'll create something YOU think is amazing about once a month. What your audience thinks may be completely different. Many amazing pieces of web content have been launched only to find the chorus of crickets deafening.

That shouldn't stop you from trying. If your amazing content fails, it will still be good content, or perhaps even great content. The key is to research what content your stakeholders will find amazing.

CREATE SOMETHING AMAZING

It's easy to over think your content creation efforts. You look around and all you see are videos, infographics, and animated gifs. You see them so often that, in your mind, it's all tired and overplayed. You dismiss ideas because you've seen them done time and time again. Except, your stakeholders likely haven't. Just because you've seen a hundred or more infographics, doesn't mean that your audience has gotten bored with them as well.

The key is to create something that is amazing for your brand. Something that will amaze your audience. Kmart's video didn't become a viral hit just because it was risqué and juvenile-YouTube is littered with such efforts. It was a hit because no one expected it from Kmart. To Kmart's stakeholders it was new, fresh, and amazing.

AMAZING IDEAS

So what are some amazing content ideas that you can try? Here are some examples of how others have amazed their own centers of influence.

Infographics—When Avalaunch Media wanted to showcase its infographic creation services, it faced a crowded field. To stand out, the company took every single popular cat meme (think Grumpy Cat) and created an infographic that matched a different cat to a different social media channel. The infographic was a big hit and Avalaunch Media picked up big name clients such as Verizon and The Home Depot in the process.

Animation—Overit is a twenty-year-old digital marketing agency out of Albany, New York. The company offers a full range of promotion and marketing services, but it knows that it competes in a crowded field. To stand out from the crowd, Overit uses its own in-house animation and motion graphic team to create amazing animated cartoons and videos to attract new clients such as Marvel and Donald Trump's own line of vodka.

Blog posts—Most of your good content will be in the form of a blog post or white paper. Turning this written medium into something amazing is what Copyblogger Media does best. Compelling headlines such as "7 Things the Great Copywriters Wish You Knew" and "Are You Still Playing Russian Roulette with Google?" backed up with equally insightful advice, have helped the company go from a simple blog to a highly successful software and training organization.

Tools—You don't have to create a sophisticated piece of software in order to build a name for yourself. Scott Stratten, the popular author who is often referred to by his online nickname "Unmarketing," took his reputation to a new level when he created the "No" button. Actually, it's technically called the "Noooooooooooooooo.com" button. Over three hundred thousand people visit the website each month simply to click on a big blue button that plays the audio of Darth Vader saying "no." With over forty thousand tweets and half a million Facebook likes, it's safe to say that many people find it to be amazing.

MAKE AMAZING CONTENT SHAREABLE

Now that you're working to create amazing content, you need to think about where it benefits you most to have it shared. Some social sharing will happen on its own, but you're also going to have to do your part to funnel the sharing to the social networks that best serve your goals and best target your centers of influence.

You need to herd your audience.

TODAY'S EXERCISE

Write down any amazing content that has caught your attention. Are there any opportunities for you to create something similar?

FUNNEL YOUR FANS

"Choice might be appealing as a theory, but in reality, people might find more and more choice to actually be debilitating." —**Sheena Iyengar**

YOU'VE CREATED SOMETHING amazing and you're ready to share it with the world. You click publish and then... nothing. You check your web analytics and your social media monitoring dashboard and... still nothing. It's one of the most deflating feelings in social media marketing and you're not the first person to experience it. The good news is it doesn't have to be that way. You shouldn't give up on your amazing content, you just have to help your audience discover and share it.

MAKE IT SHAREABLE

The first step in getting your amazing content shared is to make it shareable. Your carefully crafted blog post is not going to get shared much if it's paragraph after paragraph of text, with no visual stimulation, and a title that only its mother could love. If you want your amazing content to be shared, you have to think like your target audience. What would make them want to share it?

For written content, a catchy headline means that someone tweeting your post doesn't have to think twice about what to say. You've helped them out by creating a headline that is interesting, engaging, or mysterious. When you add an image or two to your post, you make it easier for someone to share it on Pinterest because now they don't have to hunt around for an image to add to their Pin. And when you add bolding to key points or use bullet points instead of a wordy paragraph you capture the attention span of busy professionals on LinkedIn.

The Internet is a time suck and you don't want to add to that problem. By making sure your amazing content can be shared quickly and easily, you increase your chances that it will be shared via one of the many social networks out there.

BE SOCIALLY SELECTIVE

There are literally hundreds of social networks where your amazing content can be shared. If you're not careful, you could end up with a smorgasbord of social media buttons all vying for the attention of an audience that is already inundated with requests to share what they've read, watched, and heard with their network of friends. Show them a dozen different social sharing icons and they'll just stare at them like a deer in the headlights, and end up not sharing at all.

Instead, display only those social media icons that best match your circles of influence. If your stakeholders don't tend to hang out on Reddit or Digg then don't use those buttons on your content. If you're actively trying to reach more people on Twitter, then make sure that you include a button that makes it easy for them to tweet what you publish. WordPress publishers can find many plugins that will let you customize what social sharing buttons are displayed on each post. For other web pages, you can quickly install sharing buttons using a service such as AddThis.com or ShareThis.com.

Lastly, be sure to place your most important social sharing buttons first. If your main focus is to get more Facebook likes, then place that button ahead of any others. It sounds trivial, but the order in which you line up your social sharing buttons can make a difference in where your content is shared the most.

DON'T RELY ON SHARING BUTTONS

While placing the social sharing buttons next to your amazing content will help spread it around the web, you shouldn't rely on your audience proactively clicking them. Sometimes it takes some extra effort to get those initial retweets or likes. You can give your amazing content a chance to enter the realms of social media glory by using some of the following tactics:

Suggest it—Don't just place social sharing buttons around your content and hope that someone will decide to click on one of them. At the end of your post or during the closing credits of your video ask your audience to share it with their friends. Sometimes politely asking is the impetus they need to share it.

E-mail lists—Here's something that you know to be true, but likely overlook: just about everyone who uses social media also has an e-mail account. When you publish your amazing blog post, viral-ready video, or link-attracting infographic, make sure you e-mail it to those who subscribe to your blog or to customers who have given you permission to contact them. At the bottom of that e-mail, ask them to consider sharing it with others if they found it useful. E-mail marketing services such as MailChimp.com make it easy for you to add social sharing buttons to your e-mail messages.

Boost it—Twitter and Facebook are just a couple of social networks that provide options to sponsor your content and it give an artificial boost. Spending $20 to give your content a quick boost might just be enough to get the ball rolling and the likes flowing.

Ask for a favor—I'll admit that there are times that I worry that the latest piece of amazing content I created will not gain much traction. That's when it can be helpful to have a group of close industry friends and peers you can reach out to privately and ask if they might consider tweeting, liking, or commenting. However, that generally only works if you've earned enough social currency to cash in with them.

EARNING SOCIAL CURRENCY

Forget Bitcoins. The hottest virtual payment system doesn't have a platform for trading and spending. Instead, it relies on something that people have been using in business for hundreds of years: goodwill. Goodwill is what you will use as your social currency to help increase the sharing of the amazing content you've worked hard to produce.

Goodwill is earned when you unselfishly look to help those in your centers of influence. It's earned when you tweet the post of an existing customer. You bank goodwill when you help one of your peers out by giving their latest video a thumbs-up. Goodwill also increases when you spend time sharing great content that doesn't benefit you in any way but adds to the value of your stakeholders. Think of that one person you know who is always helping others. Always sharing things that help you do your job better. The person who you would jump through a fiery hoop to help out. That person has a lot of goodwill.

Goodwill is the social currency that helps make your amazing content become viral content. You earn it by not trying to actively earn it. In other words, you build a reputation for being a person or brand that is relentless in helping others to be better.

When you earn that reputation you'll earn a lot of goodwill. Then you'll find that when you publish that amazing content, you can cash in some of that social currency by asking others to help spread the word. Earn enough goodwill and you won't even need to ask. Your stakeholders will relish the opportunity to help you out.

Over the next four chapters you'll learn how to build up a ton of goodwill.

TODAY'S EXERCISE

Pick no more than four social media sharing icons and start placing them next to any content you publish.

THANK YOUR SUPPORTERS

"The only people with whom you should try to get even are those who have helped you." —**John E. Southard**

THERE ARE TWO words that are vital to include in your vocabulary if you wish to build a better online reputation. The first is "sorry" and the second is "thanks." Later in this book you'll learn how to say sorry when you mess up—yes, there are best practices for apologizing. Today's focus is on the importance of thanking your supporters and the tremendous benefits that come from showing your gratitude.

GIVE THEM A RETURN ON INVESTMENT

People want to feel appreciated for their generosity or kind words. While you should never do something nice for someone just to earn their praise, there's no doubt that all of us appreciate it when a kind gesture earns us a "thank you." So why is it that in social media we often overlook this simple token of appreciation?

When someone takes the time to share your press release, tweet out how much they love your company, or leaves a kudos-filled comment on your blog post, it takes just a handful of seconds to reply with a simple "thanks." When you do so, you demonstrate that you don't take their public praise for granted. You signal to them your understanding that their endorsement just helped you to raise your reputation a little.

Saying thank you is so important to your online reputation, I want to spend some time walking you through how to find praise, how best to respond, and some pitfalls to avoid.

EYES WIDE OPEN

Whether you've decided to use a social media monitoring tool or are focusing your efforts on your centers of influence, you should keep your eyes wide open for any form of praise.

If you've done your homework, then you're already an active participant in the social networks where your stakeholders tend to hang out. This means that most of the kudos shared about you will be done so directly with you. A customer will tweet using your @username or perhaps they'll post a glowing review directly to your Facebook wall and not their own personal one. That's awesome! That direct interaction makes it easy for you to identify that a thank you is in order.

Just as likely, someone will share your amazing content or mention your latest video, without directly bringing you into the conversation. That's when a social media monitoring tool earns its keep, by alerting you to a conversation that you might otherwise have missed. You now have an opportunity to engage that person and thank them for their reputation-boosting comment.

HOW TO SAY THANK YOU

Hopefully some of you just read the above heading and mentally asked, "Do we really need to be instructed on how to say thank you?" If you did, you're one of the smart ones. Unfortunately, far too many individuals and companies overlook not only how to say thank you, but how best to do it. With that in mind, here are some techniques you can use to express your gratitude:

Twitter—For the most part, you need simply to reply to the tweet with a brief thank you. If you're fortunate, you may earn the love and affection of someone that tweets about you often or retweets you on numerous occasions. You don't have to say thank you to each instance, but then again no one ever complained for being thanked too much!

Facebook—Again, a reply to a Facebook post or comment with a note of thanks will always earn you reputation points, but even just the act of clicking "Like" signals that you appreciate what was written.

Blog Comments—If someone writes a blog post that includes praise for you then you've hit the reputation jackpot. The post doesn't have to be on the Huffington Post or USA Today in order for it to help build your reputation. At the very least leave a comment thanking them for their kind words. One step better, why not share that post via your own social networking channels? The author will appreciate you amplifying their audience and it helps spread the kudos to other key stakeholders.

E-mail—There's no cost to send an e-mail to someone. It takes less than a minute to send an e-mail to the person who just bragged about you online. It shows your appreciation while cementing his or her positive sentiment towards you.

Personally—If you ever bump into your supporters in real life, don't miss the chance to thank them in person. I once sought out a Trackur fan at a conference and specifically stopped him to thank him for all the retweets and social sharing he does of our online content. Paying for lunch or dinner is another easy way to express your gratitude to someone who's helped grow your reputation.

A note—What's the value to your reputation if someone writes a glowing review about you? I bet it's worth at least sending a thank you card, a handwritten letter, or a small gift.

A WORD OF CAUTION

Before you rush off and start thanking everyone who has ever mentioned you online, there are a few areas of caution to which you should pay attention. First, while it's okay to share someone's praise with your own network, do so sparingly. Too much retweeting or Facebook sharing of someone's praise can appear as though you are bragging and lack humility. There's no hard and fast rule, but reserve the re-sharing for the praise that others won't blame you for wanting to share.

In addition, tread carefully when joining conversations about your brand where you weren't directly invited to join in. A J.D. Power & Associates survey shows that consumers are still not sure if they want you to eavesdrop on their conversations or not. It's roughly a 50/50 split between those who want you to join in and those who find it to be creepy.

Now that you have a better idea of how to go about thanking those who share praise for your reputation, let's take a look at how we can generate that positive buzz in the first place.

TODAY'S EXERCISE

Go and thank someone for his or her kind words and make it your new daily habit to do so.

BETTER PRESS RELATIONS

"There is only one thing in the world worse than being talked about, and that is not being talked about." —**Oscar Wilde**

AS SOMEONE WHO has been blogging for over ten years, I'm still shocked by the number of horrible press pitches I receive each and every day from supposedly public relations professionals. They often start out like this:

> *"Dear Blogger,*
>
> *We know you write about the widget industry and thought you might be interested in the latest announcement from John Doe, CEO of Acme Widgets. He has just announced... "*

I use the fictional "John Doe" name because most press pitches are practically dead on arrival in my e-mail inbox. No personal salutation, no attempt to show they actually read my blog, and who the heck is this CEO anyway? Why should I care what he just announced?

When you consider just how important a news article or blog post can be to your online reputation, you'd think PR pros would do a better job with their initial outreach. Well, you're going to learn how to build buzz for your reputation. You're going to learn how to conduct press outreach the *Repped* way!

BUILD A PRESS LIST

On Day 6, you took steps to identify influential bloggers and journalists covering your industry. If you've not already done so, build a list of those who you think might eventually have an interest in you and what you have to tell them. Use your social media monitoring tools to track articles and blog posts that specifically mention your competitors or your industry in general. While it's tempting to build out a list using journalists who appear to have the largest audience, focusing on *The Wall Street Journal* caliber writers is not always the best approach. They're often too busy and too focused on Fortune 1000-size companies to write about what you or your organization is working on.

Instead, pay attention to the niche bloggers and trade journalists who seem to cover your industry or have written about one of your competitors in the past. You should even Google the name of one of the companies they've written about previously and see if their article shows up on the first page of search results. That's a publication that can help you most with your reputation efforts!

FOLLOW THEM

The next step is to follow them via any social media channel they appear to be the most active. Even if their centers of influence are not perfectly aligned with yours—they are popular on Twitter, but that's not your main focus—follow them anyway. You'll learn a lot about the stories they like to cover, the angles that appear to get their attention, or the type of pitches they most complain about.

After a few weeks of getting to know these people, start sharing what they publish. Tweet their latest article. Share their blog post on one of your social networks. You'll accomplish two things. First, you'll get on their radar in the best way possible—you're helping them to share what they've written—and second, you're sharing interesting and valuable content that your own network will appreciate. A double-rainbow of reputation winning!

YOUR FIRST CONTACT

Science fiction novels are littered with instances of the human race's first contact with an alien species leading to the annihilation of our planet because of some communication faux pas. How you first reach out to a journalist or blogger will set the tone for the entire relationship. If your first e-mail or tweet to them is all about you, then it will likely end in disaster. Congratulations, you just caused the destruction of earth!

Instead, make your first contact all about them. Send them a developing story that you spotted on Reddit or Hacker News. Praise them for their latest article and describe how much it has helped you and your business. Don't fake the praise. Be sincere. If you can't honestly find something nice to say about what they have written, then they probably shouldn't be on your outreach list from the outset.

When you contact them without any pretense or press pitch, it disarms them. A popular journalist might receive a dozen generic press pitches a day. Your e-mail asking only that they keep up the great writing will likely stand out and make their day.

PITCHING THE *REPPED* WAY

When you do finally make your first pitch to them, try the following approach:

1. **Use a succinct subject line.** Make the subject of your e-mail as amazing as any other content you create.

2. **Use their first name.** We all love to hear and read our own name. Use theirs in your salutation.

3. **Make a connection.** Either connect your e-mail to one you sent previously, or suggest that you have something that may be of interest to them based on something they previously wrote.

4. **Make it brief.** Use your Twittervator training to explain what it is you would like to share with them and why they might find it worth writing about.

5. **Offer something exclusive.** If you can, offer the exclusive for your news. If that's not possible, then try to offer something that will be in part exclusive—a product demo, for example.

6. **Ask if they are interested or not.** End the e-mail suggesting that you will be in touch the next day to see if the story is of interest to them or if you should share it with someone else. That way they know that you'd like to hear back from them either way.

All of this should be shared in an e-mail of less than two to three short paragraphs. Now is not the time to include an attachment with the draft press release. You're trying to gauge their initial interest, not bog down their inbox. That said, keep in mind that the above outline is a starting point. It's a template you can use if you've never approached a journalist before, or have but were guilty of the John Doe approach I outlined at the beginning. You absolutely need to follow and learn about a journalist before you contact them. If they happen to mention that they only look at press pitches if the press release is attached to the e-mail, then by all means adapt your outreach accordingly.

Done correctly, you'll gain their attention and before you can say, "We come in peace," they've written about your news and helped boost your online reputation.

IT'S ALL ABOUT BUILDING GOODWILL

As you can see, even your blogger and journalist outreach doesn't happen without first building up some goodwill. The common theme is to look for ways to be of help to those who can have a positive influence on your online reputation.

The next step is to delight your customers so that they too can't help writing about you.

TODAY'S EXERCISE

Follow the bloggers and journalists who can help grow your reputation and start connecting with them.

ALWAYS BE HELPING

"Courteous treatment will make a customer a walking advertisement." —**James Cash Penney**

I ABSOLUTELY LOVE receiving tweets like this one:

"Just experienced fantastic customer service from @andybeal @trackur social media monitoring tool, much appreciated."

When a customer takes the time to tell his or her Twitter followers that your company provided a great customer experience, it's reputation gold. When you consider how readily customers take to social media to complain, any time you're the recipient of unsolicited praise, you should savor the moment—or mark the tweet as a favorite, like I did.

STAND OUT FROM THE CROWD

You don't have to be Nordstrom or Lexus in order to provide your customers with excellent service. Sure, taking back a customer's return of used car tires—when you don't even sell car tires—will ensure your place in customer service folklore, but to delight customers enough that they can't help telling their friends, family, and social networks doesn't need to take some kind of herculean effort on your part.

In most cases, earning yourself the generous praise of your customers often only takes being better than your competitors. At Trackur, we don't have a toll free number and we don't assign each customer with a project or campaign manager. Most of our customer inquiries are handled automatically by our FAQs, and our software is so easy to use we receive relatively few customer support tickets at all. How we're able to stand out from the crowd is by making sure any contact we do have with our customers goes above and beyond their expectations. Just like Avis, we try harder.

EXCEED CUSTOMER EXPECTATIONS

There are many different ways you can provide a great customer service experience, most of which won't cost you an arm and a leg—or a set of new car tires. The key is to understand how your stakeholders are likely to reach out to you and then make sure that experience goes smoothly and, whenever possible, goes beyond the experience they expected.

When you can do that, you increase the chances that a customer can't help wanting to tell the rest of the world how much you rock. Let's look at some ways you can delight your customers into helping you build a better online reputation.

TELEPHONE

The biggest frustration most customers have when calling you is that they don't know how long it will take to get an answer to their question or a resolution to their problem. Discover Card's current TV ads do a great job of resonating with tired consumers by showing that, when you call their toll free number, you get straight through to a live person.

When someone calls you for assistance make sure that any automated navigation is only one level deep so that they reach a real person quickly. When connected, take their name and number early on, just in case they get disconnected and so that you can personalize the call by using their name. Lastly, be transparent with any steps that you need to take before being able to answer their question or resolve their issue. By telling them how long the call should last, what it is you need to do in order to assist them, and what outcome they can expect, you will go a long way toward easing any apprehension and increasing the chances they'll finish the call more than satisfied.

E-MAIL

Using e-mail for customer service is a great way to serve many customers at once, without the cost of an expensive call center. Unfortunately, e-mails are notoriously hard to track and customers can get lost between the virtual cracks of your mailbox. Instead, use a company such as Zendesk.com to add structure to your e-mail customer service. Using a dedicated e-mail address, Zendesk will turn e-mails into tickets, which can be tagged, assigned, and tracked from submission to resolution.

LIVE CHAT

The multi-billion dollar software company SAS is such a believer in live chat that it has an entire team dedicated to providing instant online customer service. Live Chat is a great way to provide quick answers to easy questions and can often remove a stumbling block in a sales process, or help clarify how to get the best out of your product or service. The good news is that, thanks to affordable solutions such as Olark.com, you don't need deep pockets or an IT team in order to offer live chat customer service.

SELF SERVICE

Providing your customers with self-service tools is crucial. Many of us are too busy to waste our time on the phone or wait for an e-mail response. Your customers are smart and often tech-savvy enough to find the help themselves. By providing a frequently asked questions (FAQs) page or customer forum, many customers will get the answers they need and then move on.

Whenever you start seeing the same question asked over and over of your customer service agents, look for the opportunity to create an FAQ or forum post that provides the answer. After a few weeks, check your web analytics and determine if there's any question or help article that gets a lot of customer visits. Those are the opportunities to improve your product so that your customers don't have to scratch their heads in frustration in the first place!

SOCIAL NETWORKS

Some social networks lend themselves to customer service better than others. Twitter and Facebook are both great platforms for answering quick questions or as a method of escalating to a support ticket. YouTube and Instagram? Not so much. If your customers tweet you a question, try to answer the best you can within any restrictions of the channel in question. If you find that you need more than 140 characters to provide help, direct them to your customer service platform of choice, but don't forget to close the social network loop by later asking if they received the help they needed.

CLOSE THE LOOP

Closing the customer service loop is important, no matter which method you use to provide customer service. Don't take it for granted that the support you provided met with the satisfaction of your customer. The last thing you want is to see a tweet or blog post claiming that you weren't interested in helping. Instead, follow up shortly after your believe the request has been resolved and make sure the customer feels the same way. Zendesk.com offers this as an automated customer service survey and will let you know if a customer isn't satisfied with your response.

WHEN THE GOING GETS TOUGH

Most of your customer interactions will involve pleasant customers with easy questions about your company or its products and services. Unfortunately, they won't all be that easy. Some customers will want you to compare yourself to your biggest competitor, while others will seem like they're asking such difficult questions, you'll wonder if they actually *are* your biggest competitor. On Day 16, you'll look at how not to respond to difficult customers and their questions.

TODAY'S EXERCISE

What steps can you take to make sure your customers don't fall through any customer service cracks?

DON'T TALK TRASH

"Never make negative comments or spread rumors about anyone. It depreciates their reputation and yours." —**Brian Koslow**

THERE'S A REASON why online reputation management has become so important. The rise of social media has made it easy for anyone to take to the web and share their opinion about anyone or anything. Sometimes those opinions are a deliberate attack and sometimes it's just a simple case of wanting to vent. Let off a little steam.

The problem for you is that it can be tempting to do just that when dealing with a difficult customer or annoying competitor. An off-the-cuff tweet about a customer, a Facebook post about your boss, or blog comment about one of your competitors might seem benign, but can quickly escalate into a reputation crisis you didn't see coming.

DON'T TRASH-TALK

The problem with talking smack is that your attempt to devalue the reputation of someone else often backfires against you. Unless you're an NFL quarterback or WWE wrestler, talking trash makes you look petty, desperate, or just plain ugly. It doesn't even matter if you trash-talk in a private forum or behind a protected Twitter stream, this stuff tends to leak out. There you were carefully crafting the perfect brand and now your own words have tarnished your reputation.

In the movie *Bambi*, the character Thumper is reminded, "If you can't say something nice, don't say nothin' at all." Great advice that's worth exploring in more detail.

DON'T TALK TRASH ABOUT YOUR COMPETITORS

As you grow your reputation, you'll find yourself on the radar of more and more stakeholders. These people will undoubtedly have questions about why they should trust, and do business, with you. Inevitably, you'll be asked how you stack up to your competition. Be careful, it's a trap!

While you should know how you match up to your biggest competitors, you should also know how best to relay that information without it appearing as though you are trash talking. The key is to play to your own strengths in such a way that it highlights your competitors' weaknesses.

If you're comparing yourself to your competition in general, then you'll want to pick two or three talking points where you know that your reputation is the strongest. If you're asked to compare yourself to a specific competitor, then you can be more specific in the areas that you wish to highlight. Saying, "We offer the best battery life of all tablet manufacturers," sounds a whole lot better than, "Have you seen how awful the battery life is for Competitor X's tablet?"

If nothing else, talking trash about your competitors is a distraction. First, you allow yourself to be compared to another person or company. Don't let their brand become a part of your reputation positioning. Second, how far are you willing to go with this? What if your competitor starts talking negatively about your brand? What if they get so annoyed with your comparisons that they start running display ads attacking your brand? Not only can trash talk become a drain on your time, but it can also drain you financially.

DON'T BADMOUTH YOUR CUSTOMERS

Please tell me the above sub-heading is causing you to scratch your head and ask, "Why would anyone trash-talk their own customers?" I hope that this seems obvious to you, but you would be surprised how often it happens.

The problem occurs when you send obscure tweets about that "difficult customer" or tell your Facebook friends about "a really annoying client that is an idiot." Your attempt to be vague and ambiguous can easily ruffle some feathers. How easily? All it takes is for your customer to be a Facebook friend or Twitter follower. They just got off the phone with you and now they see your comment. You don't think they'll put two and two together?

DON'T TRASH TALK YOUR BOSS

As I am writing this, over two dozen people have tweeted out "I hate my boss" in the past twenty-four hours. What were they thinking? They have publicly tweeted how much they dislike their superior, so I am assuming that they want to get fired this week.

Google+, Facebook, and Twitter are littered with employees publicly venting, without realizing that their manager could easily be monitoring their social media activity. If you want to badmouth your boss, confide with your best friend over coffee at a coffee shop at least five miles from your place of work!

YOU'RE NOT ALWAYS RIGHT

Another good reason not to talk-trash is that you never know when you have all of the facts. You may gripe about how a customer keeps complaining that your software constantly crashes. You tell your social network that the customer is a troglodyte, only to later discover a bug in your software that is indeed causing it to crash.

You should always give others the benefit of the doubt. It is much safer to assume the customer has a genuine problem instead of later backtracking and eating humble pie because you called someone a moron. Better yet, don't trash-talk them at all, and never have this problem in the first place!

THE EXCEPTION TO THE RULE

Hopefully you're now convinced why you should never trash-talk online. With that rule firmly planted in your mind, it's time to break it. There is one exception where it can be permissible—and even beneficial—to trash-talk your competitor or customer. The exception can be made when you are under a defamatory reputation attack. If you are facing unfair accusations then you absolutely need to be vocal and stick up for yourself.

You'll learn more about handling such unsubstantiated attacks on Day 28. For now, stay focused on talking about your positive attributes and stay away from trash-talking others. That's advice so easy a cartoon rabbit can understand it!

TODAY'S EXERCISE

Make a list of your strengths so you can focus on those when asked to compare yourself to your competitor.

EARNING TRUSTED REVIEWS

"There is place in the world for any business that takes care of its customers-after the sale." **—Harvey MacKay**

AS MUCH AS 85% of consumers say that they read online reviews about local businesses and 73% of them say that positive customer reviews make them trust a business more *(source: BrightLocal)*. It's the same for online businesses, with 74% of consumer electronics shoppers searching out online reviews before they make a purchase *(source: Weber Shandwick)*. It doesn't matter what industry you are in or how you conduct your business, your customers are checking out online reviews in an effort to judge whether to trust you or not.

There are review sites that rate individuals, companies, non-profits, products, doctors, real estate agents, employers, and even lovers! Online reviews are an important part of your efforts to get *Repped* and today you'll focus on making sure yours is worthy of five stars!

NOT ALL REVIEW SITES ARE EQUAL

Just like your other circles of influence, there are some review sites that matter more to your online reputation than others. If you're an author, Amazon will likely be the review site you care most about. A coffee shop owner might focus on Yelp reviews, while a plumber should care what rating Angie's List gives him. For hotels and resorts, a TripAdvisor review can make or break your occupancy levels.

No matter what your industry, it's practically guaranteed there's a popular review site that's already rating your reputation. The key is to funnel your customers to leave their reviews on the sites that will help you the most with your reputation efforts. The best way to do that is to provide an experience that they can't wait to tell others about.

ENCOURAGING POSITIVE REVIEWS

The number of businesses that rely solely on online review sites as a means to collect customer feedback always surprises me. That's a risky gamble to take with your reputation. What if the customer has a bad experience? Do you really want to learn about it first via a Yelp review? The time to influence a customer review is before that customer ever gets to the computer. If you're not interacting with your customer before they've completed their transaction with you, then you're playing Russian roulette with your ratings.

Instead, build in points of contact with your customer along every step of their relationship with you. I've stayed at a hotel that welcomed me with a note from the manager and his cell phone number in case of any issues with my stay. I've received a personalized thank you e-mail from a CEO asking me to contact him if ever there's a problem with my website hosting. And a local mechanic sent me a thank you card for letting him fix my car.

Find a way to connect with your customer directly and make a positive impression. That way, if your customers have a problem, they reach out to you first, not the review app on their smart phone!

HANDLING NEGATIVE REVIEWS

Do enough business transactions and eventually you'll get your first negative online review. While it can be disheartening to receive a 1-star review, all is not lost. How you handle the review can make a big difference in how it's perceived by potential customers who happen to read it.

There will be many times when the best response is no response at all. In addition, some review sites discourage responses (GoodReads) while others provide an official platform for responding (TripAdvisor). If you feel one is warranted—perhaps to diffuse a customer complaint—then the following four steps will help you craft your response.

Thank them—Thank the customer for taking the time to leave the review. It shows there is no animosity on your part and that you appreciate the opportunity to do better.

Accentuate the positives—Highlight any of the positive remarks they've made about you. This helps anyone reading your reply to see that doing business with you wasn't a completely negative experience.

Apologize for the negatives—This is not the time to make excuses, but it is the time to explain any mitigating circumstances and to suggest that this is not the normal experience enjoyed by your customers, clients, or guests. By apologizing, you send a signal to everyone that this is below your normal high standard of excellence.

Take it offline—Assuming you're able to post your comments to the review—not all review sites allow that—you should attempt to take the remainder of the conversation offline. Provide your e-mail or telephone number, or a link to your customer support page. Let this customer know that you want to ensure he or she is happy, while at the same time sending a message to prospective customers that, should they have a similar problem, you won't leave them up any proverbial creek without paddle.

After that, endeavor to improve the experience for the next customer. The above approach will only work if the negative reviews appear to be isolated incidents. If you're continually responding to 1-star reviews, then perhaps it's time to fix the underlying issue.

REVIEWS BY YOUR COMPETITORS

What happens when you receive an unfavorable review where the facts don't quite add up? They say they ate dinner at your restaurant on a Sunday, but you don't open on Sundays. Or perhaps they accuse your product of having a faulty power cable, but it hasn't even shipped yet. Likely it's a competitor trying to undermine your review rating by posting seemingly real, but totally unsubstantiated, reviews.

When this happens it's important to collect as much information as you can to confirm any discrepancies in the review. In addition, look for blatant recommendations for a competitor's alternative product or service. Lastly, check out the reviewer's profile and see if this is the only review they have written or that they've trashed all competing products except for one—which they can't help gushing about.

When you're convinced that you're dealing with a review written by a competitor, your best next step is to send the information to the review site owner. Some review sites will have a formal means of doing that, while others might require you to send an e-mail or use the general contact form. If the review isn't removed after a few days, you can generally reduce its credibility with a reply along the lines of:

"We'd love to be able to resolve this matter for you, but we've not been able to verify that this transaction took place. Could you please contact us directly so we can collect more information and make sure we turn this experience around?"

You'll likely never hear from them again and anyone else reading their review will do so suspicious of its authenticity.

DON'T FAKE REVIEWS

Like any aspect of your reputation management you may get frustrated that the needle is not going in the right direction, or things are not improving fast enough. While it may be tempting, don't ever think about posting fake positive reviews.

Whatever cunning plan you've created, the review sites are likely already one step ahead of you. Using different computers, building up fictitious reviewer profiles, asking your friends to chime in, and spacing out your reviews are all tactics that have been tried by others in the past. Even if you can get a few fake reviews past any automated spam filters, you still run the risk of getting found out. In October, 2013, Samsung was reportedly busted and fined over $340,000 for its involvement in building fake reviews for its products (source: news.cnet.com).

AN AUTHENTIC RATING

A perfect 5-star rating doesn't get you too far if you have only a handful of total reviews. As you add more reviews, you'll naturally attract some that are 3- or 4-star and even those with the best reputation attract their share of 1- and 2-star reviews. The key is to build an authentic-looking review profile. If you have a couple hundred reviews, a few low ratings may mean you slip from a perfect score, but they'll also help convince others that each positive review is genuine.

It's more important to have an authentic 4.1-star rating than a fake 5-star one.

TODAY'S EXERCISE

What are some ways you can better connect with your customers so they share any complaints with you directly?

AUDITING YOUR GOOGLE REPUTATION

"Search without Google is like social networking without Facebook: unimaginable." —**Evgeny Morozov**

OVER THE NEXT four days of Repped, you're going to work on improving your search engine reputation. Search engine reputation management (SERM) is generally the most important part of any online reputation management campaign. It's virtually impossible to go a single day without using Google, Bing, Yahoo, or even DuckDuckGo (yes, there really is a search engine called that).

When it comes to SERM, you should focus all of your efforts on what shows up in Google's search engine results pages (SERPs). With Google holding a healthy 88% global market share (source: StatCounter), anyone conducting research on your reputation is likely going to start at Google.com. Unlike the wild west of the late nineties and early two thousands—when the search engines couldn't agree on the best way to rank a web page—they now use pretty much the same ranking factors. The bottom line? If you can clean up your Google reputation, then you should also find your reputation on the other search engines will improve.

CREATE A BENCHMARK

Before you start optimizing your website and tweaking your social media profiles, it's important to know your starting point. How does your Google reputation look today? If you don't know the baseline for your SERM efforts, then you won't know how much of an improvement you've made. With this in mind, your first step in improving the SERPs for your reputation is to take a look at those results and conduct a reputation audit. Acting as a benchmark for your success, a Google audit will also show you any threats or opportunities to your reputation.

CONDUCTING YOUR GOOGLE AUDIT

The first step in your audit is to open up a spreadsheet and create columns labeled Rank, URL, Page Title, Status, and Sentiment. After that, type your name, company, product, etc., into Google and review the results. Remember to use the Incognito mode you learned about on Day 5.

Fill out the spreadsheet with the first thirty results shown by Google; enter each piece of information under the corresponding column:

Rank—What number ranking is the page in Google's search results?

URL—What is the URL of the web page?

Page Title—What is the headline displayed for that web page?

Status—Mark this either Own, Control, Influence, or Third Party. Own is something you host yourself. Control is a site only you can publish to, but is owned by someone else (e.g. your Twitter account). Influence is a page that you cannot directly update (e.g. a business partner's profile of you). Lastly, Third Party is a page where you cannot change the contents or is about someone or something with the same name.

Sentiment—Use Positive for something you would want a customer or future employer to see. Negative, is something you hope they never see. Use the label Neutral for any web page that is either benign or about someone else with the same name—it exerts neither a positive or negative influence over your reputation.

When you are done, use your spreadsheet's highlighter tool and highlight any result you've listed as positive with green. Anything negative with red, and any neutral results with yellow. This will help you more readily identify the positive from the negative results.

To download an example of how this audit should look, please head to http://www.andybeal.com/audit

UPDATE IT OFTEN

Once you've completed your audit, you should have in front of you a table that shows the first thirty Google results, color coordinated to help you identify the threats and opportunities to your reputation. The search results will change often—sometimes daily. With that in mind, you should aim to update your spreadsheet at least once a month. You may find it beneficial to create a new spreadsheet each time, so you can keep track of any improvements you've made to your Google reputation. If you get to the point where your reputation is under attack, then you will likely need to update the spreadsheet weekly or even daily.

THE 80/10/10 RULE

Now that you have a better understanding of the current state of your reputation in Google, you can focus your efforts on the positive pages you wish to push up and the negative pages you wish to suppress, or push down. Generally, your goal should be to see all green for the first ten results in Google. Few searchers will dig deeper than the first ten results, so long as they don't see anything negative about you.

When deciding which of the web pages to optimize and, hopefully, improve upon their Google ranking, you should keep in mind the 80/10/10 rule. The 80/10/10 rule is designed to ensure that your Google reputation tactics are applied to the web content that will benefit you the most. Here's how it looks:

Spend 80% of your effort on web content you own—those items that you fully control, are hosted on your server, and cannot be edited by anyone but yourself. Those pages in your audit marked Own are the ones that you will spend most of your time optimizing.

Spend 10% of your effort on web content you control—any social media profile (e.g. Twitter or Facebook) or any blog not hosted by you (Wordpress.com or Blogspot.com) will fall into this category. While you are the only one who can update the page, you are also at the mercy of the provider going out of business or deleting your account for violating its terms and conditions.

Spend 10% of your effort on web content you influence— examples of this type of content include profiles of you published by a business partner, or a listing in a business or local chamber directory. You can ask for changes, but you cannot apply them directly.

The 80/10/10 rule is designed to help you concentrate on the web content that will always be around to help shape your reputation in Google. By spending less time on pages not directly owned by you, you minimize the risk that your hard work will evaporate overnight because you failed to comply with a social network's user policy, or because that hot social media start-up runs out of cash and shuts down.

ROLL UP YOUR SLEEVES

Now that you have a clear picture of your Google reputation, you can start working on optimizing and improving those pages that will help you put forward the best reputation possible. If you find yourself staring at a lot of red on your spreadsheet, you may think it's going to take a superhuman effort to improve your reputation. Don't worry. Superbrand is to the rescue!

TODAY'S EXERCISE

Audit the first thirty results for your Google reputation.

SUPERBRAND TO YOUR REPUTATION'S RESCUE

"With great power comes great responsibility"

—Spiderman's Uncle Ben

THERE'S A GOOD chance that you are already number one in Google's search results for your name, especially if you followed the steps outlined on Day 9. The reason you are at the top of the pile for your personal or company name is that you likely own yourname.com (or some variation), your website includes plenty of mentions for your name, and other websites and profiles all link back to you using your name. As dumb as Google's search engine spider can be, it's at least smart enough to know that when someone searches for your name, your own website should be listed first, or at least pretty close to first.

When your own website ranks first for your brand, your SERM efforts get just a little bit easier because Google knows that no other site in its index is more relevant to your reputation. This extends to products and service names as well and also applies whether you're focusing on your company or personal reputation efforts. Effectively, Google makes the declaration that no other page in its index is more relevant to your name than the one you own.

Google declares you the Superbrand.

THE SUPER-WHAT-NOW?

Okay, so Google doesn't have an official "Superbrand" designation and you won't see a red cape show up against your website in the search listings. While being a Superbrand won't allow you to fly or see through walls, it will bestow upon you one very important power that will help you in your search engine reputation efforts: the ability to pass on credibility to any website you link to that is also relevant to your name.

How does that work? As number one in Google for your name, you can link to your blog, social media profile, photos, or videos and effectively vouch that they are relevant to your reputation. As the owner of AndyBeal.com, if I link to my Twitter profile at Twitter.com/andybeal, I send an important signal to Google that the profile is relevant and endorsed by me. You don't have to add any hidden code or complete a request with the wonks at the Googleplex. You just link from your site to the site that you are trying to help rank for your name. However, there is one vital component to help make this work the best for you.

OPTIMIZE THE ANCHOR TEXT

The phrase "anchor text" refers to the visible, clickable text that's displayed on the page when linking to another web page. In its simplest form, the anchor text might say "Click here" or "Visit our blog." The actual link may point the browser to company.com/blog, but the text that the user clicks is something different. That same anchor text gives direction both to the web page visitor and to Google's spider.

To take advantage of your Superbrand status, you will need to optimize your use of any anchor text that points to a page that you would prefer rank higher in Google's search results. Optimizing this anchor text is not a complex task. It merely requires that you use your reputation instead of some generic text.

Let's say Toyota wanted to improve the Google ranking of its Facebook page when someone searches for "Toyota." The company is already number one in Google, so its name "Toyota" is a Superbrand. Instead of linking to its Facebook page using the anchor text "Find us on Facebook" it could use the anchor text "Follow Toyota on Facebook." Now, when Google's spider "crawls" the Toyota website, it will see a link pointing to the Facebook page. It will also see that "Toyota" is included in the anchor text. The link itself and the optimized anchor text will send a strong collective signal to Google that the Facebook page is highly relevant to Toyota, and therefore should be shown prominently whenever someone searches for the car manufacturer.

The same approach works equally well for pages within the same website. Instead of using the anchor text "About Us," it could use "About Toyota" and point the link to a page that is hopefully already well optimized using the tactics discussed on Day 9.

SPREAD THE LOVE

Now that you have a basic understanding of how you can optimize your anchor text, you should put it to good use. Any time you want a page to rank higher for your name, consider using your Superbrand powers and include your name in the anchor text. When you link out to your social media profile, look for a way to include your Superbrand. If you issue a press release include a link back to your news page using your name in the anchor text.

The key is to find ways to include your brand in the anchor text of any page you identified as important to rank on Day 18. If you own the page, control it, or at least influence it, then build some links to it using your Superbrand in the anchor text.

There are two important caveats. First, you shouldn't use only your name in the anchor text. A hundred links all using the anchor text "Toyota" don't help your visitors or Google in the long run. Instead, look to mention your Superbrand alongside other descriptive words. For example, "Check out the Toyota Pinterest board."

Second, you should only use this approach in any deliberate efforts to help the recipient page to rank higher for your name. If you're trying to get a web page to rank for "Orlando real estate" you should use that phrase in any anchor text pointing to it, not "Bob Smith's real estate."

IT'S NOT A MAGIC BULLET

While I wish I could tell you that using your Superbrand in your anchor text is all you need to focus on, in order to improve your Google reputation, it's not quite that simple. While optimizing your anchor text will help Google understand the relevance of the recipient web page, when it actually visits the page, it still needs to be convinced that the content is indeed important enough to show on the first page of any results when someone Googles your name.

That's why the next step is to make sure you link out to web pages that have the best chance of ranking in the first ten results of Google.

TODAY'S EXERCISE

Identify any existing links that could be changed from generic anchor text to something that includes your Superbrand.

---

http://

CONTENT THAT ROCKS GOOGLE'S WORLD

"We want Google to be the third half of your brain." —**Sergey Brin**

USING YOUR SUPERBRAND powers will only get you so far in your efforts to push positive web content higher up in Google's search results. To maximize the benefits of your optimized anchor text, you need to consider the quality and relevance of the web page to which you are linking. Link to a page that uses pronouns in lieu of your name, or doesn't have your brand in the URL, and you're going to make your Google reputation management efforts more difficult than needed.

Instead, focus on those web pages that you either *Own* or *Control*, are already showing up in the first thirty Google results for your name, are positive in sentiment, and match up with your centers of influence. These are your top candidates for on-page optimization and to receive the benefit of your Superbrand links. If you're struggling to find enough existing web pages that match your criteria, then you may have to repurpose existing web content or build new pages to help you take control of your Google reputation.

OPTIMIZE YOUR EXISTING DOMAIN

Just because your own website is the Superbrand, that doesn't mean it's working 100% to help your Google reputation. While your homepage may sit at the top of the search results, you may be missing out on the opportunity to push other pages from your website into the top ten results.

Generally, your "About Us" page is the perfect candidate for this task, but any page on your site, relevant to your personal or company name, can work. Make sure the page heading includes your name, the description is in the third person, and that any menu link to the page includes your Superbrand in the anchor text. With these in place, you should find that Google starts ranking the page right below your existing homepage listing.

UTILIZE YOUR OTHER TLDS

I bet if you check your domain registrar account, you'll rediscover an existing top-level domain (TLD) that you registered a long time ago, but never used. That ".org" or ".net" TLD can be put to great use with some careful planning.

There's nothing that says you can only use your ".com" domain name in your reputation strategy. Many large corporations already use multiple TLDs to host specialized content, so the approach is not new. Take an existing TLD—or register a new one—and use it to host web content that can be safely separated from your existing website. A great example would be for a blog or consumer portal. Microsoft protects its Google reputation with additional domains such as MicrosoftStore.com and I use this tactic by separating my professional blog (andybeal.com) from my personal, more whimsical blog (andybeal.me).

After you optimize the content on your other TLDs you should see that they quickly gain favor in the eyes of Google—especially if you link to them! There are only two caveats to this approach. First, don't duplicate any content that is already published on your existing website, and second, don't go overboard adding TLDs— build out one or two at most!

THE BENEFITS OF SUB-DOMAINS

Another great approach is to make use of the unlimited supply of sub-domains available to you. Unlike a TLD, which requires a registration fee, sub-domains are free and you're not restricted by existing availability.

What is a sub-domain? It's easier to show you than to explain it to you. For example, help.trackur.com is a sub-domain. So is play.google.com. That word in front of the TLD means that the company has created a sub-domain that piggybacks off of the authority of the main domain name, but is treated by Google (and your browser) as a completely separate website.

Sub-domains don't require a registration fee and you can name them whatever you wish. For your reputation management efforts you'll create one or two and use them for anything from your careers center, to your investor portal, to your blog. A few pages of carefully optimized content, a link from your existing website, and it should start making its way up Google's search results.

NOT ALL SOCIAL PROFILES ARE EQUAL

While it is true that you should focus your reputation efforts on those social media networks that help you to best reach your centers of influence, there are some that will rank better in Google than others.

Any time you can customize your social media bio or profile page, you increase the likelihood that Google will display that page prominently in its search results. Twitter, Facebook, LinkedIn, and Flickr are just a few of the social networks that will let you create a profile, customize the URL (see Day 9) and write a bio about yourself—in the third person, of course! And, don't forget to link to each one using your optimized anchor text.

DON'T OVERLOOK VIDEOS AND IMAGES

While it is true that text heavy web pages tend to do better in Google's search results, you shouldn't overlook the importance of images and video in your reputation management strategy. The search engines are getting smarter at understanding all types of web content, and Google in particular loves to display images and videos alongside traditional text results.

Create a YouTube channel and upload a tour of your office, demos of your products, or even customer testimonials. Label everything with your name—the channel, the video file, the video title, the video description, and the video tags—and your videos will start showing up in the search results. Even if they don't show up in Google, YouTube is technically the second largest search engine on the planet, so you'll at least put forward your best reputation to those searching for videos about you!

For photos and images, you should check out Flickr.com. The Yahoo owned photo-hosting site carries a lot of authority and its images often show up in the search results. Again, make sure every label includes your name and you'll make it easier for Google to find a flattering headshot or professional product image.

WHAT ELSE RANKS?

All of the above suggestions fall into the *Own* or *Control* categories on your Google audit spreadsheet. They are ideal candidates for optimization as you're able to maximize their potential for ranking in Google's top ten. The next step is to look at how your Google reputation can benefit from content that you can only *Influence*.

TODAY'S EXERCISE

Brainstorm content that you could move from your main website to either another TLD or a sub-domain.

THE COMPANY THAT YOU KEEP

"Associate with men of good quality if you esteem your own reputation; for it is better to be alone than in bad company."

— **George Washington**

YOU'VE PROBABLY EXPERIENCED an "I wish they hadn't have done that" moment at some point in your life. Whether it was a friend posting a raunchy photo to your Facebook wall, or a business partner caught ripping off its customers. At some point, those you associate with will do something that causes a knot in your stomach and results in you taking a metaphorical step to the side, nonchalantly whistling as you try to disassociate yourself from their actions.

While the behavior of those around you can rub off on your own reputation, that's not always a bad thing. In fact, for your Google reputation efforts, your friends, partners, investors, and associates can help you immensely.

FRIENDS WITH BENEFITS

There are only so many of your own web pages that Google will display when someone Googles you. The search engine looks for diversity in its search results, which is why on Day 20 you optimized social profiles, videos and images, in addition to your own web content. To further help the search engine's spider, it's time to rally those with whom you do business, or associate yourself, and encourage them to publish positive web pages about you.

When others publish positive content about you, your Google reputation benefits in two ways. First, the content they create is about you. Therefore, as long as it is optimized, it provides Google with yet another page to show searchers when they Google you. Second, if you can also get them to link to your website—or better, one of your sub-domains or social profiles—those links will push those pages higher up in Google's SERPs.

In case you're struggling to come up with ideas for finding partners who can help you, here are some to get you started.

BUSINESS PARTNERS

Many companies will list their business partners somewhere on their website. Unfortunately, your name in a long list of other names is not going to help you much. Instead, ask your business partner if they would mind creating a page on their site that focuses on how you benefit each other, and your customers, by partnering. You could even suggest that you write it for them, so as to save them the time and effort. That way, you can make sure that the page URL, heading, content, and links are all optimized.

SPONSORSHIPS

If you sponsor a trade event or industry conference, you should find that your dollars secure you many promotional benefits in return. The next time you sponsor an event, negotiate that the organizers also include a page on the event's website with your profile. It should include your name, personal or corporate bio, and a link back to your website. Congratulations! You just provided Google with yet another topical web page to display in its search results!

NON-PROFITS AND ASSOCIATIONS

I bet there are at least a handful of groups that ask you for a donation each year. Perhaps you donate your time to the local shelter, or write a sizeable check to your alumni association. You should be commended and your prime motivation for doing this should always be to give back.

That said, why not inquire as to any opportunities to be featured on the group's website? Perhaps they could write a blog entry about all that you do to help. Maybe they'd be willing to create a profile page recognizing your years of loyal support. If they agree, you've not only provided the search engines with a new page for its index, but one that shows your charitable spirit. That will do wonders for any online reputation!

AFFILIATES

If you don't already have an affiliate program, you should seriously consider one. It doesn't have to be a complex or require the expensive assistance offered by Commission Junction or

LinkShare. We created one for Trackur and discovered an amazing side benefit.

Not only will affiliates work hard to refer new business to you, but the smartest affiliates do one very clever thing: they write about you. They realize that the best way to get people to click on their affiliate link is to write a review of your company or product. When they do, they provide Google with a fresh source of web content, one that will likely be very positive. After all, they want to earn their commission, right?

GUEST POSTS

Writing a guest post that will help your company's reputation is tricky. If you make it too much about your company, it will likely be rejected by the publisher for being too self-promotional. However, for individuals, guest posts offer a two-fold benefit.

Most guest posts include a space for an "About the Author" section. This is not something you should leave up to the publisher. Write it for them, so that you can optimize it for your name. That way, it increases the chances that Google will display one of your guest posts when someone searches for you. The other benefit is that writing guest posts helps to build your reputation as an expert in your field. Even if they do not readily show up in Google, they become something you can point others to when they ask about your background and general expertise.

CO-BRANDING

The last tactic that can help create positive content for Google is co-branding. Co-branding has been around for decades. Two companies come together to piggyback off of each other's reputation and cross-promote to each other's stakeholders.

A very smart way to use co-branding for your Google reputation management is to work on a joint contest or sweepstakes. The benefit comes when your contest partner shares details of the giveaway with their audience. They'll mention your name, they'll likely write a blog post—or perhaps issue a press release—and spread the contest to their various social networks. You both build a reputation for being a generous company that loves its stakeholders and some of that goodwill will spill over to Google's search results.

THE IMPORTANCE OF BEING PROACTIVE

As can see from the past couple of days, it's important to be proactive in building your Google reputation. In the absence of any positive content you've created, Google will fill the void in its search results with anything that it finds relevant—even if it is something negative. The best defense is offense and taking the time to mold your reputation now will better prepare you for when your reputation comes under attack.

And it will come under attack.

TODAY'S EXERCISE

Make a list of existing business partners you can reach out to and ask for a profile page on their websites.

CHAPTER 22

KNOW YOUR REPUTATION'S WEAKNESSES

"Once we know our weaknesses they cease to do us any harm."

—Georg C. Lichtenberg

AT SOME POINT in your career, you'll stare down the most infamous interview question of them all: What are your biggest weaknesses? If you're like most job candidates, you'll have prepared an answer that takes a pseudo weakness and turns it into an apparent strength. "My biggest weakness is that I care too much about people." That may be great for job interviews, but that kind of response is not going to cut it in reputation management.

While you may not ever want to reveal your biggest weaknesses to a hiring manager, when it comes to your online reputation, you absolutely need to identify and own your weaknesses. The alternative is to go about your business blissfully unaware of your reputation's Achilles' heel or worse, know your weaknesses, but deny they'll ever present a problem. Well, research firm Oxford Metrica would like you to know that there is an 80% chance your company will lose at least 20% of its value at some point over the next five years (source: Reputation Review 2012).

Do you still want to ignore your reputation's weaknesses?

DISCOVER YOUR WEAKNESSES

While many reputation crises involve some kind of self-inflicted harm—a rogue employee's tweet, or crass Facebook post—the biggest threat comes from being blind-sided by an attack that focuses on your biggest weakness. To ensure that you are better prepared, it's vital that you identify those areas of vulnerability before someone else does.

If you spend the time to take an honest look at the way you conduct business, it should become apparent where you are weak. If you find yourself struggling, then ask others for their thoughts. Your employees, coworkers, customers, or business partners can all provide an impartial opinion on where they feel you are most weak. Be sure to ask enough people so that you can discover any commonality among the feedback. If more than a handful of people identify the same weakness, then you can bet at some point it will become the target of someone intent on attacking your reputation.

LOOK TO YOUR COMPETITORS

One of the best ways to identify your own weaknesses is to look at those of your biggest competitors. Any time you see a rival face an attack on his or her reputation, use that as an opportunity to identify if the same weakness exists for you. If it doesn't, great, you just discovered another "strength" that you can highlight when talking to prospective customers (remember highlight your strengths, don't talk trash about a competitor). If you discover you actually share your competitor's weakness, then you can be thankful for two reasons. One, the attack happened to him or her and not you. Two, you can take steps to insulate your reputation from a similar attack.

BE ON ALERT

Once you've identified your reputation's weak spots, the next step is to make sure your reputation monitoring is set up to alert you to any specific mention of them. Unless you're a distant relative to Nostradamus, you can't possibly foresee the focus of your next reputation attack, but you can certainly take steps to make sure you are monitoring for those that might target your weaknesses.

A great idea is to send any reputation alerts that mention your weaknesses to a priority destination. While it may be okay that all general reputation alerts go to an intern who checks them once a day, Monday through Friday, any alert that includes a known weakness shouldn't get lost in the mix. Instead, set these alerts to go to someone who has the authority to act, even on a weekend. If needed, use a specific e-mail address that makes the person's smart phone light up like a Christmas tree! Just make sure someone sees it.

PREPARE YOUR RESPONSE

Another big benefit of knowing your reputation's weaknesses is that you can take a few steps to prepare for an attack. By knowing where your reputation will most likely come under fire, you can prepare talking points or even take some steps to preempt an attack.

If you know your latest camera suffers from poor battery life, make sure you prepare talking points that explain that it's to be expected in order to achieve all of the other great features it offers. If your company doesn't offer telephone support on the weekends, make sure your customers know that this allows you to offer prices that are much lower than your competitors. If you can take your weaknesses and contrast them with your strengths, your stakeholders will be less likely to attack you over them.

REMOVE THEM FROM THE EQUATION

The best way to protect your reputation from its weaknesses is to remove those weaknesses from the equation. Once you know your biggest failings, you can spend time and effort on ways to improve upon them.

When Motorola released its flagship Moto X phone it was praised by critics for everything except its camera. Every review of the otherwise excellent smart phone was marred by negative comments about the absolutely awful photos it took. Motorola listened, and just a few months later, released a software update that dramatically improved the quality of the photographs taken with the device. The Moto X is no longer criticized for having a weak camera.

Admittedly, you won't always be able to fix your weaknesses and there's still the issue of inadvertently self-inflicting damage to your own reputation. That's why on Day 23 you'll learn the three most important components of a reputation attack safety net.

TODAY'S EXERCISE

Make a list of your weaknesses and set up specific monitoring for them.

YOUR REPUTATION SAFETY NET

"Vulnerability is the first thing I look for in you and the last thing I'm willing to show you." —**Brene Brown**

BACK IN 2008, the popular pain reliever Motrin discovered that its online reputation never takes a day off, when hundreds of moms took offense at a YouTube campaign the company launched on a Friday. Unfortunately, no one at the company saw the backlash until Monday.

Fast forward to 2013 and you would think companies would have learned a lot in those five years—like, your reputation doesn't clock out on Friday and then back in on Monday. Nope! When a British Airways passenger needed assistance over the weekend, he reached out to the airline using Twitter. Unfortunately, his requests for help went unanswered so the customer decided to seek revenge by purchasing a sponsored tweet which read:

"Don't fly @BritishAirways. Their customer service is horrendous."

That sponsored tweet caught the attention of more than just that customer's 500 Twitter followers. Many news outlets picked up the story and it went viral faster than a BA flight from London to New York! When BA did finally respond, they tried to explain that their Twitter feed shuts down for the weekends. Yes, you read that correctly. Despite offering flights 24/7, a website that is accessible any hour of the day, and operators standing by to take your call, BA decided that they could just turn off their Twitter monitoring each weekend!

YOUR THREE-STAGE MONITORING PLAN

Your reputation never takes a day off. Sure, you might need a little R&R, but that doesn't mean you can stick your head in the sand until you're back in front of your computer. You need to monitor your reputation at all times. Fortunately, there are three different approaches to reputation monitoring which, when combined, should protect you from being blindsided by a weekend rant.

AUTOMATED SOCIAL MEDIA MONITORING

If you're not able to schedule time to check on your social networks on a regular basis, then it is vital that you use an automated social media monitoring tool. Back on Day 5, you looked at the different types of social media monitoring platforms available to you. If you haven't already set one up, now is the time to do so. Pay particular attention to any tool that allows you to receive real-time alerts for any conversations about your reputation—especially those with a negative vibe.

YOUR WEB ANALYTICS

When someone publishes a negative blog post about your company, tweets discontent, or gives you a tongue-lashing on YouTube, there's a good chance you'll see a spike in your web analytics. When an angry customer goes on the attack, his or her audience gets curious. That audience wants to take a look at the recipient of the detractor's onslaught, so they visit your website.

Most of the time, you'll see referrals directly from the source of the outrage. A spike in traffic from a domain name that you don't recognize, or an increase in the number of visitors from Twitter. Other times, you may just see an overall increase in direct visitors to a specific page on your website. If someone complains to his or her e-mail subscribers about your stance on a particular sensitive issue, then you might see an influx of visitors landing directly on the blog post or press release page related to that topic.

You should check your web analytics at least once day, even if it's only for reputation management reasons. If you can't commit to that, then either assign the task to someone else or look for a web analytics solution that will e-mail you an alert if something out of the ordinary shows up in your website traffic.

YOUR STAKEHOLDERS

Many years ago, the company I worked at became the recipient of a rather ugly attack on an industry message board. Way before I would ever have discovered it, an industry friend dropped me an e-mail to let me know. Thanks to the help, I was able to join the conversation, correct some inaccurate information, and de-escalate the situation, all before lunch.

This is where building goodwill (Day 12) can really benefit you. When you build a great reputation among your stakeholders, they will be eager to help you out in times of distress. When they see your name come under attack, they'll send you an e-mail, a direct tweet, or a private message. Why? They've bought in to your brand; they've become a stakeholder. And while those who are upset might be quick to call you out, those who think you are doing a great job will want to stick up for you.

One of the keys to fostering this behavior from those who support you is to let them know how much it is appreciated. Even if you were already aware of the situation, don't brush them off with a cold response—or no response at all. Always take time to thank them and, if they really saved your butt, perhaps send them a thank you card or small gift. They'll know you appreciate the support and will practically trip over themselves to help you again, should they see another attack.

Awareness is the first step of a reputation attack. Over the remaining chapters of *Repped*, you're going to learn how to respond to an attack, how to clean up the mess, and how to ensure it doesn't happen again.

First, you need to understand the people behind the attack.

TODAY'S EXERCISE

Create a system for monitoring your reputation during the weekend. Perhaps learn from doctors and service technicians and set up an "on call" weekend rotation.

IDENTIFYING YOUR DETRACTORS

"If my critics saw me walking over the Thames they would say it was because I couldn't swim." —**Margaret Thatcher**

JUST AS EACH reputation has its stakeholders, so too it will have its share of detractors. While not always welcomed, detractors are still stakeholders, in that their opinions and actions contribute to the overall perception of your online reputation. Although it is impossible to identify and classify every single person who attacks your reputation, you should find that many fall into at least one of the following seven categories.

THE LOYALIST

Loyalist detractors know your brand very well. They're likely long-time customers and have spent many years, and many dollars, buying from you. They know what to expect from your reputation and they have a keen sense of any departure from your normal service or product standards.

When Loyalists make a complaint, you should give them special attention. They've spent a lot of money with you and, if you don't keep them happy, could decide to take their future transactions elsewhere.

American Airlines does a great job of keeping its Loyalists happy with its AAdvantage frequent flier program-rewarding its "elite" fliers with additional perks and priority customer service.

THE BRANDVOCATE

Brandvocates have not only invested their dollars, but also invested their time as an advocate for your brand. They love you! They tell others just how great you are and, without any monetary incentive, refer a lot of customers your way.

Brandvocates will feel the most slighted when you make an announcement that they feel they should have been consulted on. When the apparel retailer Gap tried to change its logo, its Brandvocates quickly attacked the new design and caused the company to make a quick retreat.

The best way to keep your Brandvocates happy is to set up an insider's club or newsletter where they receive exclusive sneak peeks at new products and have their chance to provide feedback before you make any changes to your brand.

THE VIRGIN

The Virgin is represented by all of the customers doing business with you for the first time. They had an expectation of how you would treat them and you didn't live up to that.

Virgin detractors will most likely complain when they feel suckered. Perhaps your sales representative over-sold the fuel efficiency of your trucks, or your latest laundry detergent didn't get out the toughest stains, as promised.

Keep your Virgins happy by recognizing that they may need their hands held a little more. Follow-up calls after a purchase, a new customer onboarding process, and not over-selling in the first place, will all help avoid a reputation attack from a Virgin detractor.

THE PROFESSIONAL

You can open the shades again; Professional detractors are not hired hit men. Instead, they represent anyone who writes reviews or critiques for a living. Journalists, bloggers, and secret shoppers all fall into this category of detractor.

A reputation attack by Professionals will likely be more tempered, but that is offset by the wider audience they enjoy. Famed technology columnist Walt Mossberg might not ever fervently attack your reputation, but if he remarks that your new computer is too slow to compete with its rivals, then millions of people will be influenced by his criticism.

Building relationships with your Professional detractors is the best way to avoid the worst of their attacks. A continual feed of honest information, an effort to make yourself available to answer their questions, and talking points that explain your weaknesses, will all go a long way to softening their blow.

THE DISGRUNTLED

Believe it or not, your own employees can do just as much damage as any other type of detractor. Disgruntled employees may well try to anonymize their attacks, but their secrecy can often lend insider credibility to their words.

Disgruntled detractors will often leave anonymous comments on blog posts about you, or write reviews under a pseudonym. For the most part, they'll cover their tracks, but you'll know that the attack is coming from the inside by the startling accuracy of their claims.

While it's important to monitor what your employees say in social media, even more important is to ensure that your employees are actually happy. Keep them trained, keep them challenged, pay them well, and ultimately make them feel that they are an important part of your reputation. When they feel that way, they'll be less likely to attack the same reputation they are invested in.

THE UNDERMINER

Not every detractor is exactly who they claim to be. An undermining detractor is very likely a competitor out to sabotage your online reputation.

Underminers will be deliberately vague in their complaints. You'll read their review and something—or a lot of things—just won't add up. You can't find their order or that rude employee named "John" doesn't even exist. It doesn't matter to Underminers. Their goal is to leave enough negative reviews that your potential customers will start to question your integrity.

The best method for dealing with Underminers is to offer a toll free number or e-mail address where they can reach you. Express your desire to get more specific details so that you can rectify their situation and you should find that they quickly lose their voice and scurry back to the shadows of the Internet.

THE TROLL

The Troll lives for the reputation attack. An employee you fired for stealing, a customer who felt you didn't rectify a situation satisfactorily, or perhaps even a jilted lover. The Troll represents anyone who delights in sabotaging your reputation.

Trolls are practically impossible to please. They don't want anything from you and by engaging them you only fuel their flames of critique and give them the audience they so desperately desire.

For the most part you should ignore the Trolls. As Scott Stratten reminds his Twitter followers, you are not the "Jack Ass Whisperer." While it may be painful to leave their comments unanswered, you'll likely find that most stakeholders will ignore their incoherent rants. Only if they drift over to the realm of defamation should you pay attention—something you'll learn more about on Day 28.

ONE SIZE DOESN'T FIT ALL

A detractor can fall into any of the aforementioned categories. You may even find some overlap—a Brandvocate who also writes as a Professional for the local newspaper or a Disgruntled employee acting as a Troll. You may not even be able to readily define your detractors. If that's the case, try to look for patterns in their complaints, or look at reviews they've left for others. Someone may look like a Professional, but upon further digging you realize that he works for a rival and always attacks his competitors.

Having an idea of the different categories of detractors will mean one less thing to figure out, when staring down a bona fide reputation attack.

TODAY'S EXERCISE

Create a plan to keep your Loyalist, Brandvocate, and Professional detractors in the loop and invested in your reputation.

THE FIRST STEPS WHEN YOUR REPUTATION IS UNDER ATTACK

"Everyone should be quick to listen, slow to speak and slow to become angry." —**James 1:19**

IT'S HAPPENED.

Someone has published a negative review about you, and it's ugly. Reputation damaging, pass the aspirin, this is going to be a long day, ugly.

When you first learn of an attack against your reputation your stomach will turn somersaults and your palms will get sweaty. Like a Category 5 hurricane, a reputation attack can sweep through and do a lot of damage. However, just like a hurricane, there are steps you can take to prepare for such an attack. Steps that will help you keep a clear head and limit the amount of damage to that great reputation you've worked so hard to build.

DON'T PANIC

The first step is to not panic. Easier said than done, right? Take a few deep breaths. If needed, step away from the computer and pour yourself a cup of coffee. Whatever it takes to get over that initial reaction that makes you want to, as they say in Internet slang, fix all the things!

Because you took time to set up your social media monitoring you've likely caught this attack in its early stages. Just like a malignant tumor in your body, early intervention exponentially increases your chances of turning the situation around.

IDENTIFY YOUR DETRACTOR

Who are you dealing with here? Is it a Virgin detractor who ordered the wrong product and simply needs a free exchange? Or, are you staring down the blogging barrel of a Professional? Once you identify the type of detractor, you can start planning the type of response that is best warranted.

You should also try to figure out who they are as a person. What's his name? Where does she work? Can you match the person up with an existing customer record? Is the attack from a journalist you've spoken with before? Lastly, how can you reach out? Can you use Whois.com to look up a telephone number or is the only means of connection via the contact form on the detractor's website or a direct message on Twitter?

CHECK THE FACTS

The next step is to read carefully your detractor's side of the story. Make a note of the key complaints. Write down the facts and timeline of any events. What are the claims? What accusations have been made?

It's important to remain calm while you collect this information. You may be infuriated by the claims, telling yourself, "There's no way this is true; we'd never do that!" Or you may have the opposite reaction and assume that all the claims are 100% true.

While you will be tempted to reply immediately, it is far better to take a few extra minutes to compare the detractor's side of the story with reality—or at least your perception of reality. Otherwise, you may find yourself offering an apology and a refund for something that didn't even happen.

CHECK THEIR DEMANDS

If the complaint is coming from someone who has done business with you, then he or she will likely list desired compensation. If you've caught this early enough, that may be nothing more than an apology. If you've royally messed up, then the person may want a refund or compensation of some kind. Whatever the demands, they've probably been listed out for you.

If the attack is coming from a Professional, an Underminer, or a Troll then you probably won't see any demands. From a financial perspective this is good news, but it also means that finding a resolution will be no easy task. You may have to assure journalists that the bug they found will be fixed in the next software update, or find a way to reveal the true motives of an Underminer.

CHECK THEIR INFLUENCE

Next you should try to build up a profile of your detractor's audience reach. How influential are they? If they're complaining on

Twitter, use Klout.com to show you how influential they are and on what topics. How many Facebook friends do they have? Who are they connected to on LinkedIn? If they've published their attack on a website, free tools at Moz.com, Alexa.com, and MajesticSeo.com can help you figure out how many visitors they receive and which websites link to them.

While you don't want to ignore a complaint simply because the detractor has no audience, you also don't want to go overboard with your response and inadvertently create a Streisand Effect, either (http://en.wikipedia.org/wiki/Streisand_effect).

CHECK THE CONVERSATION SPREAD

Once you've identified your detractor's influence, you should check to see if his or her audience has embraced the attack on your reputation. A complaint by a Troll may fall on deaf ears because of any lack of credibility or a Professional review is ignored because it's way off from the normal topics covered by the blogger.

Conversely, if you see a lot of retweets, a healthy number of likes, or other bloggers and journalists picking up the story, then you know that you need to take steps to de-escalate the situation as quickly as possible.

SEEK TRUSTED COUNSEL

As part of your evaluation, you would be wise to seek the input of those you trust. Before you face a reputation attack, make a list of one or two people who would be willing to look at the information you have collected and give an opinion on how best to respond.

These trusted advisors should already know the reputation you are trying to build and have an understanding of your character, voice, and weaknesses. Who you include is up to you. Some suggestions include: A trusted industry peer. A business mentor—one who's successfully faced his or her own reputation challenges. Your legal advisor. Even your friends and family—some of the best advice I've received has come from the sage, levelheaded counsel of my wife.

You should try to reach them quickly and provide them with as much information as you know. Listen to their advice, but remember that this is your reputation, not theirs. Ultimately, how you respond is your decision to make.

TO RESPOND OR NOT RESPOND

By now, you have a clear understanding of the detractor; the complaint, the demands, the influence, and conversation spread. The next step is to decide how you wish to respond. You may conclude that a response is not merited at this time. That's something only you can decide. If you make the choice not to respond, you should still keep a watchful eye on your detractor to make sure the complaint doesn't escalate and garner more attention—and thus warrant a reply from you.

If you do decide to respond, there are two approaches you can take. On Day 28, you'll learn how to respond to someone who is making defamatory accusations or taking other steps to falsely attack you. More than likely, you're guilty of at least some of the complaints made against you and so a different approach is needed.

Humble pie is best served while it's still warm and tomorrow you'll learn it's the best recipe for cleaning up your reputation mess.

TODAY'S EXERCISE

Create a list of trusted advisors you'll contact when facing a reputation attack.

WHEN YOU MESS UP, FESS UP

"A reputation once broken may possibly be repaired, but the world will always keep their eyes on the spot where the crack was."

—**Joseph Hall**

When Apple launched the iPhone 5 in the Fall of 2012, it took the opportunity to unceremoniously dump Google's Map app as the default and instead launched its own mapping software.

It was horrible.

Bizarre satellite images, misplaced city locations, and driving directions that were incorrect all contributed to a reputation revolt by Apple's fanatical customers and the media alike. Just as it appeared that "Mapplegate" would undo the reputation Apple had built for launching only the best software, CEO Tim Cook took a page out Steve Jobs' playbook and published a sincere apology to the company's website.

That apology was the equivalent of throwing a bucket of water on a developing fire. Cook was sincere, transparent, and acknowledged that Apple had fallen short with its own maps app. He even went as far as recommending competitors' navigation apps as a stopgap until Apple could improve on its own offering.

HAVE SOME EMPATHY

When you let down your stakeholders, be it a botched product launch or a lapse in moral conduct, it's important to act quickly and with empathy. Put yourself in their shoes. It shouldn't be hard. You've likely experienced a situation where the product you bought was a dud or a contractor you hired took shortcuts in the job. When you make a mistake, it is all too easy to get defensive, hide behind mitigating circumstances, or worse, blame anyone else but yourself. Playing a game of rhetorical chess with your detractors only prolongs the reputation attack and ends up costing you more in the long run.

Instead, when facing a reputation crisis remember these three simple words: Sincerity, Transparency, Consistency.

SINCERITY

Most stakeholders who attack your reputation want just one thing: an apology. They want you to agree that they didn't deserve to be treated poorly by your customer service team. They want you to acknowledge that when they made a good faith purchase you should have taken care to make sure your product wasn't faulty. And they want you to admit that you shouldn't have posted a lewd photo of your private parts to the Internet. Most online reputation attacks happen because at some point you not only let a stakeholder down, but you didn't apologize for doing so.

If you're going to resolve this attack quickly, then you had better apologize quickly. Not one of those "we apologize for any inconvenience this may have caused" non-apologies, but a sincere, heartfelt apology. Whether you need to include a refund, gift card, or some other financial compensation will depend on how badly you've messed up, but at the very least you should apologize. Saying "I'm sorry" has repaired many damaged reputations.

TRANSPARENCY

When your cable goes out in the middle of the Super Bowl, the last thing you want to hear is, "We are aware of the situation and are working to resolve it." What situation? What caused it? How hard are you working? And will my signal be back in time to watch the fourth quarter—or at least that cute Budweiser commercial?

When you make a mistake, your stakeholders will want to know how in the world you let this happen. This is not a time to plead your case or blame someone else. You need to be honest about what caused the situation, what measures you've put in place to ensure it doesn't happen again, and when the situation will be resolved.

CONSISTENCY

If the first two words focus on appeasing and satisfying a specific detractor—or group of detractors—this last one is something all of your stakeholders will care about. When you make a mistake it leads to greater scrutiny by those who have decided to give you a second chance. You can bet that Tiger Woods, BP, and Apple are all on a shorter leash, now that the world is aware of their respective Achilles' heels.

After you apologize, and explain the steps you are taking to prevent a further occurrence, you then have to live out your promises. You start by actually looking at what caused the issue in the first place and taking steps to prevent it from happening again. Improving your maps software or taking steps to prevent another catastrophic oil spill may be costly, but not as costly as making the same mistake twice and losing any remaining credibility.

DELIVERING THE MESSAGE

When it comes to responding to a reputation crisis, there's only one hard and fast rule on how it should be delivered: directly from the top. While it may not always be practical for the top executive to reply, it should be your goal. If not, then the response should come from someone who appears to have enough authority so as not to appear disingenuous.

The channel of delivery will vary greatly, depending on the number of stakeholders affected by the issue at hand. If a single customer is unhappy then a direct e-mail or tweet might suffice. If the attack is more widespread then you may wish to publish a blog post and then share that across your various centers of influence.

One thing you should probably avoid is conducting the conversation on a platform where you are not the host. Resolving an issue by going back and forth in a detractor's blog comments is not wise. They could delay your response, edit your words, or not approve your comment at all. Instead, wherever possible, look to move the conversation to your website, blog, or social profile. Hosting the conversation allows you to direct interested parties to your official response.

WHAT WILL IT COST YOU?

When facing a reputation crisis most people will ask, "What is it going to cost me to resolve this attack?" That's actually the wrong question to ask. Better is to ask, "What will it cost me if I don't resolve this attack?"

The information highway is littered with reputation road kill—companies that delayed their response or tried to avoid taking responsibility for their actions. Instead of admitting their mistakes and taking the financial hit needed to correct their blunder, they instead tried to sweep things under the rug. As a result their reputation never fully recovered.

You're going to avoid making the same mistake. How? By understanding the lifetime cost of a persistent detractor.

TODAY'S EXERCISE

Decide who will be the person responsible for apologizing for any reputation blunder—and no, you can't outsource it to a PR firm.

$

THE LIFETIME COST OF A DETRACTOR

"Resistance at all cost is the most senseless act there is."

—Friedrich Durrenmatt

WHEN MOST BUSINESSES look at how much it's going to cost to restitute an unhappy customer, they focus only on what it will cost today. They balk at the idea of providing a refund or compensation because, well, no one likes to give back revenue that's already on the books.

It's this reluctance to provide a refund that often causes a small reputation crisis to flare up and get worse. While superficially it may make sense to avoid this expense, in the long run you risk losing a whole lot more.

LIFETIME CUSTOMER VALUE

If you spend any amount of time in marketing, you'll eventually hear the phrase "customer lifetime value." There are many interpretations of that statement, but Wikipedia offers a simple explanation:

> *The present value of the future cash flows attributed to the customer during his/her entire relationship with the company.*

In other words, the amount of money can you expect to make from one customer while he or she has a relationship with you.

When facing a reputation crisis, you should consider not just the lifetime value of keeping this customer happy, but the lifetime cost of the customer becoming a detractor.

LIFETIME DETRACTOR COST

Let's say you have a customer who is not happy with your website hosting company because his server crashed and he lost an entire day of productivity and business. He writes a blog post about you and suggests that a refund of his past month's hosting fees would make up for his inconvenience. That amounts to $100.

You look at the request in disbelief. There is no way you're going to refund $100 for a one-day outage. You deny the request and so he cancels his service and takes his business elsewhere. You're fine with that, because you know that you can easily replace him with another customer.

As ESPN's Lee Corso would say, "Not so fast!"

Not only do you have to consider the lost revenue of your unhappy customer—the lost lifetime customer value—but you also need to consider the effect his complaint will have on your ability to attract new customers.

The blog post he wrote about you is now sitting in the top ten of Google's search results. As a result, you lose out on the business of ten new customers the following month because they fear that they will have a bad experience with your company. If you assumed they too would have purchased a $100 a month hosting plan, and stuck around for at least a year, that equates to $12,000 in lost revenue.

You lost a total of $13,200 in revenue all because you decided you couldn't afford to refund your detractor the $100 that had been requested.

THE INTANGIBLE COSTS

In addition to the lifetime cost of a detractor, you should also consider the intangible costs involved when you decide not to acquiesce to your detractors' demands.

Time—The amount of time you spend going back and forth with your detractor could be better spent on growing your business.

Distraction—You'll spend a lot of time explaining to future customers why this happened. You also run the risk that your attacker will become a "determined" detractor—a Troll that continually looks for ways to bad-mouth you.

Sleeping—You'll lay awake at night, mentally sparring with them. Thoughts such as, "I should have told him this" or "He has no right to attack us," will ebb and flow through your mind and disrupt your sleep.

Repairing—Don't underestimate how much time and money you will have to spend to clean up your online reputation. Many online reputation firms charge in excess of $10,000 a month to clean up a bad Google reputation.

Is that $100 refund starting to look a lot more reasonable yet?

INDIVIDUALS HAVE CUSTOMERS TOO

For those of you reading this book because you wish to focus on your personal reputation, this is not a chapter to skim over. While you may think you don't have customers, you're wrong. They just look different. For individuals, a "customer" is a potential employer. The lifetime cost of a detractor is a similar calculation, the difference being you calculate how much in future earnings might you lose because a company won't hire you as a result of what it finds in Google.

COME TO AN AGREEMENT

When coming to a resolution with an unhappy customer, it's important to make sure that you are both on the same page about what is expected. This is not the time to shove a non-disparagement agreement in her face or insist she take down her blog post—that can easily backfire and make the situation worse. Instead, confirm that by offering the refund, or providing the compensation agreed upon, she will consider the matter resolved to her satisfaction.

The idea is to meet or exceed the detractors' demands so that they not only stop attacking you, but they will want to go back and update their blog post or remove their negative review. While you don't want to make your offer conditional on their retraction, you can imply that you want to make them happy again so that they will want to tell others how well you handled the situation.

RESTITUTION

Most of the time it will be better to simply say you are sorry and offer your customer some kind of compensation. Not only will this avoid the lifetime cost of a detractor, but studies suggest that an unhappy customer who receives restitution will tell more people about how great you are than one who never had a problem in the first place.

The only time when it makes sense to dig in your heels and fight is when they are making defamatory remarks or using tactics to undermine your reputation. On Day 28 of *Repped* you'll learn how to handle those types of reputation attacks.

TODAY'S EXERCISE

Determine the average lifetime value of a customer so you can better understand the lost value if one ever becomes unhappy.

A REPUTATION ATTACK WITHOUT MERIT

"A lie can travel halfway around the world while the truth is putting on its shoes." —**Mark Twain**

THERE ARE FEW justifiable reasons for getting heavy-handed in social media. When you're facing a defamatory reputation attack is one of them. It's tough enough to protect your reputation from justified criticisms when you mess up, but it's just plain unfair when someone attacks your good name without merit.

A reputation attack of this kind still requires a softly-softly approach; you don't want to stir up any support for your attacker by being too heavy-handed, but that doesn't mean you can't release the hounds when warranted.

THE NON-LEGAL LEGAL APPROACH

According to the blog search engine Technorati, 94% of bloggers will retract, edit, or delete incorrect information if you contact them. That's good news; because that's the approach you should take when being defamed online. Rather than hand this immediately to your attorney and incur the extra expense, your first contact should be a direct e-mail or letter. The tone of the letter should be friendly but firm. Explain that the author of the defamatory content has made a mistake in his or her statement. Provide your detractor with correct information and explain that the continued publication of the inaccurate comments will hurt you financially.

Your goal here is to avoid putting your detractor's back against the wall. If you start out with a full on "cease and desist" letter, you may panic the person to do something that could be further detrimental to your reputation—such as trying to invoke a David versus Goliath story with his audience. Instead, a casual e-mail will suffice in letting the person know that he has made a mistake, showing him how to make things right, and subtly implying that any lack of cooperation will leave you with no choice but to pass the matter to your legal counsel and pursue litigious recourse.

DELETE, DELETE, DELETE

When making your request, it's important to spell out exactly the action you wish the defaming detractor to take. If you don't make your demands clear, then you run the risk that the author will do nothing more than post an excerpt of your e-mail to the original article. That's not good enough.

No one ever reads the retraction section of a newspaper. Okay, perhaps a few do, but only after they're done with the obituaries. It's the same with online publications—no one ever cares about the follow-up post or the footnote edit. Certainly Google doesn't care. The negative story is what garnered all of the attention, all of the back links, and all of the social shares. The negative story is what Google will show when anyone searches for you.

What you should always request is a full deletion of the defaming statements. The article, blog post, tweet, or status update should be fully deleted. That is the only guaranteed way to avoid it showing up in Google. If the detractors are not willing to delete them completely, then the next best solution is for them to be completely redacted of any defamatory statements. They should change the title of the post, remove your name from the headline, and make sure that anyone reading the page quickly understands that the author made a mistake. If you can also get them to add a "noindex" tag to the HTML, then that will instruct Google not to show the page in its search results.

TAKING LEGAL ACTION

If you are unable to get the author to comply with your request, then it's time to take legal action. A sternly worded letter from your attorney will let the person know you mean business. Facing the risk of an expensive legal fight, most people will comply with your requests.

If the detractors don't, then it's time to put the matter before a judge. Defamation laws are tricky to understand. You can't sue someone for defamation just because you didn't like the review he did of your company. A successful claim must prove that the statement was false, caused financial harm, and was made with no attempt to research the truth. If you happen to be a notable person, such as a celebrity or public official, you also have to prove malice. That's a lot of proof needed.

Assuming you can make a solid case, you'll win a court order, forcing the author to remove his libelous statements. If he won't, is unable to, or you've sued a "John Doe" because you don't know the true identity of the detractor, then your court order can be sent to Google, requesting that it remove the content from its index.

Defamation will be your strongest argument in any legal remedy, but that's not your only option. If appropriate, you can make claims for copyright or trademark infringement, but again you can't get a negative review removed just because someone used your trademark in his write up.

KICK 'EM WHERE IT HURTS

You goal is to get the inaccurate information removed from the web. While a court victory is the only guaranteed method to achieve this, it's not the only way.

Report them to their registrars—Some domain name registries have strict policies that prevent websites from making money from defamatory attacks or from engaging in criminal activities.

Report them to their hosting companies—In the same manner, check to see if the blog or news site is violating any terms and conditions of their web host providers.

Report them to their social network—While Twitter, Facebook, Pinterest, et al, might not care that someone is defaming you, if that detractor is using your own trademarked name as his or her profile name, then you might be able to gain ownership of the account by submitting evidence of your trademark.

Report them to Google—If you find that your detractor is violating Google's guidelines about search engine optimization (SEO) spam, let the search giant know. Black hat SEO practices get websites banned from Google's index every day. Likewise, if you see that your detractor is using, and abusing, Google's AdSense ads then you can submit a complaint and have those earnings invalidated. Cutting off the income of someone defaming you is one way to get compliance.

These four tactics are a last resort approach for removing defamation. While all are perfectly legal, some of your stakeholders might question you for taking such extreme steps. Use with caution.

SHARE YOUR SIDE OF THE STORY

Even if you have a strong case for defamation and you're pursuing a legal resolution, it can be many months before you are victorious. In the meantime, the inaccurate statements are out there, hurting your online reputation. If that's the case, you may decide to address the libelous statements head on.

If you decide to leave a comment on the offending blog post, or share a Facebook update with your side of the story, make it succinct and to the point. Something along the lines of, "The statements made are 100% false and we have reached out to try and provide accurate information. Unfortunately the author is unwilling to remove her defamatory comments so we regretfully have no choice but to pursue this matter in the courts." After you share your side of the story, try to avoid being drawn in any further. Going back and forth with your detractor—or her supporters—will only inflict further damage to your reputation. As George Bernard Shaw once said, "I learned long ago never to wrestle with a pig. You get dirty, and besides, the pig likes it."

WATCH FOR THE ECHO CHAMBER

Even once you secure a legal victory, your work is not done. You will need to be diligent to monitor for any reoccurrence of the inaccurate statements. The last thing you want is for a defamatory statement to become an urban legend that gets twisted and contorted until everyone assumes it to be true.

Likewise, you don't want any echoes to show up in Google's search results. If you're unable to get your detractor's attack removed from Google—because you couldn't prove defamation due to the comments being true—then you're going to have to work hard to convince Google that it shouldn't be shown in search results. How do you do that? You make sure that Google focuses only on the positive web content that you've created and on Day 29 of *Repped*, you'll learn how to do just that.

TODAY'S EXERCISE

If you don't already have legal counsel, find an attorney that specializes in intellectual property and defamation, and keep his or her telephone number handy.

CLEANING UP THE GOOGLE MESS

"Google doesn't really forget." —**Ethan Zuckerman**

IF YOU'RE UNSUCCESSFUL in your attempts to have a negative web page removed, you're going to have to use brute force. Google wants to show its users the most relevant and most popular web content for their search query. Unfortunately, that means that the negative blog post or 1-star Yelp review has just as much chance of appearing in Google's search results as your homepage or social media profile. Fortunately, Google is not quite the cold, heartless robot its algorithm would have you believe. In fact, Google has published guidelines and recommendations for those who find their search results less than favorable.

Quoting from Google's Webmaster Tools:

> *If you can't get the content removed from the original site, you probably won't be able to completely remove it from Google's search results, either. Instead, you can try to reduce its visibility in the search results by proactively publishing useful, positive information about yourself or your business.*

There you go!

Google completely sanctions your attempts to push out a negative web page from its search results. You just have to make sure you understand its search algorithm and its webmaster guidelines.

ASSESS THE DAMAGE

If you've not conducted a Google audit since you suffered your reputation attack, this is your first task. As mentioned on Day 18, your audit should cover the first thirty results that are displayed when you Google your reputation. If you don't see your detractor's attack, then you can breathe a sigh of relief, but don't let complacency set in. You should conduct a new Google audit daily for the next two weeks, then extend it to weekly for the next month or two, before settling back to your normal schedule. This process will ensure you can move quickly, should the attack start to rank inside the first thirty results.

Should you see the attack appear in your audit, you shouldn't necessarily hit the panic button. Google's algorithm includes many signals for freshness and diversity. Your detractor might show up in the top thirty results only because the web content is new and Google wants to make sure that it displays it while it figures out if it's important enough to earn its ranking permanently. In addition, the attack may well earn a boost while it's displayed on the homepage of a blog or news site. Just as a link from your own homepage provides any page a Google boost, so too a link from a publisher's own homepage will provide a hand up. It's often temporary because that link will vanish once other posts and articles are published to your detractor's homepage.

RAMP UP YOUR OPTIMIZATION

When you look at your audit, pay attention to any web pages that you Own, Control, or Influence, but haven't yet optimized. Do you see any opportunities to add a Superbrand link? Are you using pronouns in your descriptions when you could be talking about yourself in the third person?

Now would also be a good time to ramp up your efforts to publish amazing content. If you previously put off designing an infographic or a creating a new video because you decided it would be too costly, it might be time to reconsider that decision. Compare the cost of investing in web content that might rank above the negative web page versus the lifetime cost of your detractor's attack finding a permanent home in your Google reputation.

IGNORE THE 80/10/10 RULE

I know, I know. I told you that you shouldn't optimize content that you don't own. Well, desperate times call for desperate measures. Take a look at the results in your Google audit and identify any pages that are just below the negative web page. If any of them are third-party owned, then you may want to consider giving those pages a helping hand. I know that if ever I faced a reputation crisis the Andy "I'm a billionaire" Beal from Texas, might just get some extra links to his web pages, courtesy of yours truly!

BUY YOUR WAY OUT

Many online review sites are less than honorable. Poke around the underbelly of the Internet and you will find sites that post anything from unverified customer reviews to naked photos of a scorned lover. Many of these sites have some kind of "advocacy" program that, for a small fee, will ensure the negative review is quietly removed. I use quotes around advocacy because many of them are nothing short of extortion. Still, paying a sleezeball webmaster $500 to make the nastiness go away could be a lot cheaper than the amount of time, effort, and money needed to push it down in Google's search results.

On the slightly more savory side, you could always pay a blogger to carry out a paid review of your company or sponsor an advertorial on a popular news site. If you take this approach I would suggest two things. First, make sure that you fully disclose that the content is sponsored, so that you don't give your detractor another opportunity to question your integrity. Second, it's much better to consider this tactic now, before you face a reputation attack. Not only will it give the content more time to make its way into Google's SERPs, but it completely removes any suggestion that you only used this tactic so you could clean up your Google results.

HIRE AN ORM PROFESSIONAL

If you find all of this to be completely over your head, then you may decide it worth the investment to hire an online reputation management (ORM) firm. There are literally hundreds of ORM firms and consultants—all willing to take your money. Like any industry, you have large firms, such as Brand.com, all the way down to individual consultants.

Getting references from anyone you plan to hire would be great, but possibly tricky—no one wants to give a testimonial that admits her reputation was so bad she had to hire a firm to clean it up! At a minimum those you hire should explain clearly the tactics they plan to use to help you rebuild your Google reputation. If anything sounds fishy, or runs counter to what you've read in this book, walk away. There are plenty of great ORM firms so you don't need to take any further risks with your already battle-scarred reputation.

THE ROAD AHEAD

This is not going to be a quick fix. It may take you many months to fully clean up your Google reputation. Let that be a reminder and an encouragement to never let this happen again. Remember, you may be able to clean up the mess this time, but your stakeholders will be looking for consistency from you going forward. That's why you need to circle back to the core of your reputation, your character, and make an effort to be better.

TODAY'S EXERCISE

Have you created enough Amazing content? If not, now's the time to build it, not in the middle of a reputation attack.

BE BETTER

"The great difficulty is first to win a reputation; the next to keep it while you live; and the next to preserve it after you die."

—Benjamin Haydon

WHEN CANADIAN MUSICIAN Dave Carroll flew with United Airlines in 2008, he didn't expect his precious guitar to get broken. When he wrote his protest song "United Breaks Guitars" in 2009 in an attempt to get United to compensate him for his loss, he likewise didn't expect the YouTube video to be a viral hit with over 13 million views.

Neither did United Airlines.

Shortly thereafter, United Airlines spokeswoman Robin Urbanski said the company would learn from this black eye by using Carroll's video "for training purposes to ensure all customers receive better service from us."

Fast-forward to 2013 and it appears United is attempting to make good on that promise. A mistake in the airline's online booking system resulted in fares being offered for $0 plus $5 in tax for many domestic flights. Many customers jumped on the opportunity, some getting roundtrip flights to Hawaii for just ten bucks! A mistake by a United employee created an apparent windfall for its customers, but surely the airline would just cancel the tickets and issue an insincere apology, right?

Wrong! Shortly after the mistake was identified and fixed, the official United Twitter account announced:

> "We've reviewed the error that occurred yesterday and based on these specific circumstances, we will honor the tickets."

Wow! Had United Airlines actually learned a lesson about how to handle a reputation crisis? Instead of suffering the brunt of hundreds of angry customers, the company decided that the lifetime cost of so many detractors would far outweigh the expense of honoring the insanely cheap tickets.

United Airlines followed the advice of this, your last day of *Repped*: be better!

TRANSFORM YOUR CHARACTER

Much of what you have read over the past thirty chapters has been about ways to build, manage, monitor, and repair your online reputation. However, it always circles back to the quote from Honest Abe:

> "Character is like a tree and reputation like a shadow. The shadow is what we think of it; the tree is the real thing."

If you are to have any success building an outstanding online reputation then you must provide it with a foundation of excellence.

Your reputation will only ever be as good as your character. If you do not focus on how you act, how you run your business, how you build your products, you'll find that improving your online reputation becomes a game of Whac-A-Mole—just as you bop one reputation attack on the head, another one pops up.

As you study and implement the advice in this book, be alert, be focused, be committed, but most of all, be better!

CONCLUSION

JUST AS FOLLOWING a 30-day exercise plan won't immediately give you the body of Jillian Michaels, so too reading *Repped* won't immediately give you the reputation of Nordstrom or Coca-Cola. What it will do is give you a solid foundation that will help you to understand the important role your stakeholders play in the formation of your online reputation, provide you the tactics to start engaging your centers of influence, and show you how to use your Superbrand to saturate Google's search results with positive web pages.

Building a great online reputation is going to take some time, "a whole lot of precious time. It's gonna take patience and time. To do it, to do it, to do it, to do it right." Oh how I miss George Harrison. Where were we? Oh yes. A great online reputation requires your continued effort to be amazing, to provide a great experience for your stakeholders, to be diligent enough to listen for negative conversations, and to be humble enough to admit when you make a mistake. Sure, *Repped* is full of tactics that you can flip to, and implement without much care or consideration to the other chapters in this book, but that's the equivalent of doing one push-up then pulling on a pair of Spanx, instead of committing to the full 30 days.

The investment you make in your online reputation is totally worth it. You'll attract more customers, hire better employees, and won't have to spend as much on advertising and public relations. More importantly, you'll feel great about yourself because you'll know that your reputation will truly precede you—in a good way!

As the old proverb goes:

"May your Likes be plenty, your complaints few, and may all your Google audits be positive."

Okay, so I may have just made that up, but you get the idea. ;)

INDEX

ABOUT THE AUTHOR

ANDY BEAL IS the world's leading authority on online reputation management. Originally from Brighton, England, Andy made Raleigh, NC his home in 2000 and has slowly lost his English accent—much to the dismay of his American wife.

Andy has spoken at dozens of conferences around the world, including the USA, Canada, England, Australia and New Zealand. A trusted source for reputation management advice, Andy has appeared on major TV networks, public radio, and is often quoted in print publications such as *USA Today, Inc. Magazine*, and *The New York Times*. His first book, *Radically Transparent: Monitoring and Managing Reputations Online* was the first complete guide to online reputation management.

When not obsessing over reputation management, you'll find Andy behind a camera, strumming his ukulele, hitting a tennis ball, or volunteering at either the Raleigh Rescue Mission or Providence Baptist Church.

As you would expect, there are many different ways to reach Andy online:

andybeal.com
twitter.com/andybeal
facebook.com/andybealORM
linkedin.com/in/andybeal
plus.google.com/+AndyBeal1

61348403R00108

Made in the USA
Lexington, KY
08 March 2017